ALADDIN

ALADDIN

Book by Colin Wakefield

Music and Lyrics by Kate Edgar

WARNER/CHAPPELL PLAYS

LONDON

A Warner Music Group Company

ALADDIN
First published in 1996
by Warner/Chappell Plays Ltd
129 Park Street, London W1Y 3FA

Copyright © 1993, 1996 by Colin Wakefield and Kate Edgar

The authors assert their moral right to be identified as the authors of the work.

ISBN 0 85676 235 0

This play is protected by Copyright. According to Copyright Law, no public performance or reading of a protected play or part of that play may be given without prior authorization from Warner/Chappell Plays Ltd., as agent for the Copyright Owners.

From time to time it is necessary to restrict or even withdraw the rights of certain plays. **It is therefore essential to check with us before making a commitment to produce a play.**

NO PERFORMANCE MAY BE GIVEN WITHOUT A LICENCE

SPECIAL NOTE ON MUSIC
The music written by Kate Edgar for ALADDIN is required for production. Please contact Warner/Chappell Plays for further information regarding the score, availability and fees.

AMATEUR PRODUCTIONS
Royalties are due at least fourteen days prior to the first performance. A royalty quotation will be issued upon receipt of the following details:

Name of Licensee
Play Title
Place of Performance
Dates and Number of Performances
Audience Capacity
Ticket Prices

PROFESSIONAL PRODUCTIONS
All enquiries regarding repertory and stock rights should be addressed to Warner/Chappell Plays Ltd, 129 Park Street, London W1Y 3FA. All other enquiries should be addressed to the authors, c/o the publisher.

OVERSEAS PRODUCTIONS
Applications for productions overseas should be addressed to our local authorized agents. Further details are listed in our catalogue of plays, published every two years, or available from Warner/Chappell Plays at the address above.

CONDITIONS OF SALE
This book is sold subject to the condition that it shall not by way of trade or otherwise be re-sold, hired out, circulated or distributed without prior consent of the Publisher. **Reproduction of the text either in whole or part and by any means is strictly forbidden.**

Printed by Commercial Colour Press, London E7

ALADDIN was first performed at Salisbury Playhouse on 11th December, 1993, with the following cast:

ALADDIN	Elizabeth Hayward
WIDOW TWANKEY	Peter Lorenzelli
WISHEE WASHEE	Ben Fox
EMPEROR FOO WIFF PONG	Alister Cameron
PING PONG	Anthony Psaila
PRINCESS	Alex Kelly
SING SONG	Rosie Cavaliero
ABANAZAR	Tim Barron
GENIE OF THE RING	Diana Berriman
SLAVE OF THE LAMP	Tom Wu

CHORUS OF CHILDREN OF PEKING, ROYAL ATTENDANTS, WAITERS, JEWEL BEARERS and CHINESE BOGWOPPITS played by two teams of local children (Nat Baverstock, Debbie Biles, Daniel Hayes, Hal Kite, Elfie Rawlence, Kimberley Rendell, Brendan Chitty, Danielle Foster, Katie Holloway, Catherine Loyden, David Oakes, Graham Sowerby)

Director	Colin Wakefield
Musical Supervisor	Kate Edgar
Set designer	John Elvery
Costume designer	Su Bentinck
Choreographer	Francesca Jaynes
Lighting designer	Peter Hunter
Sound designer	Ian F Cross
On the book	Andy Barker
Musical Director/Keyboards	Simon Fraser
Keyboards	Christopher Seed
Drums/Percussion	Lyn Edwards

CHARACTERS

ALADDIN	(F) Principal Boy.
WIDOW TWANKEY	(M) Dame.
WISHEE WASHEE	(M) Kids' Friend.
EMPEROR	(M) Silly Baddy.
PING PONG	(M) Chinese Policeman.
PRINCESS	(F) EMPEROR's Daughter. Heroine.
SING SONG	(F) PRINCESS's Handmaid.
ABANAZAR	(M) Villain.
GENIE OF THE RING	(F) Dotty. Foil to ABANAZAR.
SLAVE OF THE LAMP	(M) Mysterious. Mercurial.

CHORUS of six children (3M 3F)

AUTHOR'S NOTE

The pantomime was written for a cast of ten adults and six children, but will also suit a larger company.

The principals doubled in the Opening Chorus, and elsewhere as specified in the text. With a larger Company, a separate Chorus, of whatever size, can be used for the Opening, as well as for fleshing out a number of other scenes (e.g.: the "Off With His Head" sequence, the Chase, the Chinese Bogwoppit Ballet, the Transformation in the Cave, the Celebration Number, Abanazar's Den and the Finale. Similarly, more Children could be used in these scenes as well as in the first Laundry scene.

The Chorus of Children is optional, but very useful.

Most of the characters are self-explanatory. The Slave of the Lamp, however, should be played by an actor (or actress) with strong physical skills: an athlete, gymnast, or, maybe, a karate expert. Preferably not a Chippendale hunk. The idea is that his magic should be in his physicality.

The optional UV scene included at the end of the script may follow Act Two, Scene Four. Please note that this sequence did not feature in the original production and is untested in performance.

NOTE ON THE MAGIC CARPET

The working of the MAGIC CARPET will depend on the stage resources available. In the original Salisbury production the Carpet was laid over the trap (an exact fit), which then rose up, supported by a pedestal on wheels. This pedestal in turn sat on the top of a 'new' trap, which was secured in the stage floor before the carpet moved away. A stagehand came concealed through the blacks to 'wheel' the carpet off (there were handles on the back of the pedestal). If the stage floor is black, the pedestal is black, and no smoke or dry ice is used, the illusion of flight can be perfect. The carpet should be top-lit only, with the other characters moving to the side of the stage for the Magic Carpet Spell — so there is no spill from their light to show up the pedestal.

There are other ways, of course, and equally effective methods can be devised with limited resources. Wires, however, are not ideal, because they catch the light.

SCENES

Title Cloth	Frontcloth (A): A Street in Peking and Aladdin Title

ACT ONE

Scene One	Palace Gardens
Scene Two	Frontcloth (B): Araby
Scene Three	Widow Twankey's Laundry
Scene Four	Frontcloth (A): Street in Peking
Scene Five	Palace Gardens
Scene Six	Frontcloth (A): Street in Peking
Scene Seven	(A) Outside the Cave (B) Inside the Cave
Interval	Frontcloth (A) and Aladdin Title

ACT TWO

Scene One	Frontcloth (B): Araby
Scene Two	Widow Twankey's Laundry
Scene Three	Frontcloth (A): Street in Peking
Scene Four	Palace Gardens
Scene Five	Frontcloth (B): Araby
Scene Six	Abanazar's Den in Araby
Scene Seven	Frontcloth (A): Songsheet
Scene Eight	Palace Gardens: Walkdown

MUSICAL NUMBERS

ACT ONE

Welcome to China	(COMPANY)
When I'm Rich	(WIDOW TWANKEY)
Off With His Head	(EMPEROR, PING PONG, SING SONG, PRINCESS)
Trot Down to Twankey's Laundry	(WISHEE WASHEE, WIDOW TWANKEY and CHORUS)
Far Away	(PRINCESS, SING SONG, ALADDIN)
Magical Day	(ALADDIN)

ACT TWO

I'm Feelin' Blue (3 stages)	(WIDOW TWANKEY, WISHEE WASHEE, SING SONG, PRINCESS)
Celebration (mainly dance)	(FULL COMPANY except ABANAZAR and GENIE OF THE RING)
Now I am A Genie	(GENIE OF THE RING)
Someone	(PRINCESS, ALADDIN)
Double-dealing Rotter	(ABANAZAR, WIDOW TWANKEY, PRINCESS, SING SONG)
Songsheet	(SING SONG, WISHEE WASHEE)
Finale: Celebration (reprise)	(FULL COMPANY and CHORUS)

ACT ONE

Scene One

The Palace Gardens.

The EMPEROR's ancient garden. Ordered, formal. Trees and topiary. Pagodas. Reds, golds, blues. A few wide steps from raised area upstage, suggesting walled gardens or avenues beyond.

Holiday atmosphere. Four traders with richly colourful barrows and baskets: fabrics and silks (Klo-Thing), jewels (Sparkli), gifts and toys (Toy Sar Wee), and fruit (Hel-Thi Eeting). Dressed out of character as Pekinese traders and customers are the actors playing ABANAZAR, ALADDIN, SLAVE OF THE LAMP, GENIE OF THE RING *(traders) and* EMPEROR, PING PONG, PRINCESS, SING SONG *(customers)* — *and Children. A full Company except* WIDOW TWANKEY *and* WISHEE WASHEE.

       Song: Welcome to China (COMPANY)

COMPANY	WELCOME TO CHINA — THE SUN IS IN THE SKY! WELCOME TO CHINA — OUR HOPES ARE RIDING HIGH THAT THIS WILL BE THE DAY WHEN OUR DREAMS WILL ALL COME TRUE. SO WELCOME, WELCOME TO YOU! WELCOME TO PEKING — JEWEL OF THE EAST! WHATEVER YOU ARE SEEKING — A BARGAIN OR A FEAST. COME ON DOWN, TO THE TOWN, WHERE THE SKY IS ALWAYS BLUE. AND WELCOME, WELCOME TO YOU! *(Instrumental/dance break)*
MERCHANT 1	TAKE A LOOK AT THIS SPLENDID KITE — A MOST UPLIFTING TOY!
MERCHANT 2	THIS PAIR OF STILTS — THE PERFECT GIFT FOR ANY GIRL OR BOY!
MERCHANT 3	LET ME TEMPT YOU WITH A PINEAPPLE, SO JUICY AND SWEET.
MERCHANT 4	A MELON OR A MANGO — A LYCHEE AS A TREAT!

MERCHANT 2	BUY MY SAPPHIRES, EMERALDS — THIS RING FROM KATMANDU!
MERCHANT 1	TRY ON THESE PEARLS FROM BABYLON — OH YES — THEY'RE *VERY* YOU!
MERCHANT 4	WOULD YOU LIKE A SILKEN SCARF TO WRAP AROUND YOUR WAIST?
MERCHANT 3	I CAN TELL IT SUITS YOU WELL, AND IT'S IN THE FINEST TASTE!
COMPANY	WELCOME TO CHINA — THE SUN IS IN THE SKY! WELCOME TO CHINA — OUR HOPES ARE RIDING HIGH THAT THIS WILL BE THE DAY WHEN OUR DREAMS WILL ALL COME TRUE. SO WELCOME, WELCOME TO YOU! COME ON DOWN, TO THE TOWN, WHERE THE SKY IS ALWAYS BLUE. AND WELCOME, WELCOME, WELCOME, WELCOME TO YOU!

(Traders wheel off their barrows. Customers also exit. Children remain, briefly playing tag. Enter WISHEE WASHEE *with laundry basket.)*

WISHEE Watcha Kids!

CHILDREN Watcha Wishee!

WISHEE *(to audience)* Watcha Kids! *(Little response.)* Hey, that wasn't very good!

(He introduces himself and teaches the routine.)

Brilliant! Now we can all be mates. Now, you may be wondering what I'm doing with this basket. Well, my Mum runs the Laundry, and I'm off to the Palace to fetch the Emperor Foo Wiff Pong's dirty washing. *(Reaction from Children.)* Yes, he is rather smelly. That's my brother's job really, but he's been in a funny mood lately. His name's Aladdin —

(Frantic whistling off. Enter PING PONG, *in a panic.)*

PING PONG Clear the streets! Don't panic! Clear the streets!

(Children run off. PING PONG *bumps into* WISHEE *and they both fall over.* PING PONG *hits* WISHEE *over the head with his truncheon.)*

PING PONG	Take that!
WISHEE	Okay! (*He takes the truncheon.*) And you take that!
	(*He hits* PING PONG *over the head.*)
PING PONG	Don't do that!
WISHEE	Do what?
PING PONG	Hit me over the head with my truncheon.
WISHEE	What?
PING PONG	Hit me over the head with my truncheon.
WISHEE	Okay!
	(*He hits* PING PONG *over the head again.*)
PING PONG	I'm looking for Aladdin.
WISHEE	Who are you, anyway?
PING PONG	PC Ping Pong, Chief of Police to the Emperor Foo Wiff Pong.
WISHEE	You're new?
PING PONG	True. Ping Pong new. Ping Pong not here long. Did belong in Hong Kong, but had big ding dong in posh restaurant. Fell headlong into egg foo yong. Ping Pong felt strong he stay in Hong Kong too long. Now belong in Peking with Foo Wiff Pong.
WISHEE	That's easy for you to say. But why do you want Aladdin?
PING PONG	He's been stealing apples from the Palace Orchard. Emperor Foo Wiff Pong humungously angry. Have you seen him?
WISHEE	Yes — he went . . . (*Clearly making it up.*) . . . that-a-way.
PING PONG	I thank you.
	(*Exit* PING PONG.)
WISHEE	Well, Aladdin may have been acting funny, but he wouldn't go around stealing.

(*Enter* ALADDIN.)

ALADDIN Watcha Wishee!

WISHEE Watcha Aladdin! Here, have you met my new mates? (ALADDIN *greets audience*.) Hey — I've just met this new policeman —

ALADDIN Not Ping Pong? The ex-Hong Kong egg foo yong ding-dong who thinks he's King Kong?

WISHEE That's the one. He says you've been stealing apples.

ALADDIN I'd never steal anything, Wishee.

WISHEE Then what were you doing in the Palace Orchard?

ALADDIN Can you and your mates here keep a secret?

WISHEE Of course we can. Can't we?

AUDIENCE Yes!

WISHEE (*louder*) Can't we?

AUDIENCE YES!

ALADDIN You know the Princess, Wishee?

WISHEE Everyone knows the Princess.

ALADDIN But nobody's ever seen her. Right?

WISHEE Right.

ALADDIN Wrong!

WISHEE Wrong?

ALADDIN Right! *I've* seen the Princess, Wishee. That's what I was doing in the Palace Orchard. She's the most beautiful person I've ever seen in my life.

WISHEE Talking of life, Aladdin. You know the punishment for looking at the Princess?

ALADDIN What?

WISHEE You get your head chopped off!

ALADDIN	I don't care.
TWANKEY	(*off*) Aladdin!
ALADDIN	That's Ma! See you later, Wishee! (*To audience.*) 'Bye!

(*Exit* ALADDIN.)

TWANKEY	(*off*) Wishee!
WISHEE	And I'm late for the Emperor's washing. 'Bye everybody!

(*Exit* WISHEE. *Enter* WIDOW TWANKEY *on tricycle with clutter.*)

TWANKEY	Wishee! Where is that boy? Wish- (*She sees the audience.*) Oh, hello dears — I didn't see you there! I'm Widow Twankey, and I'm looking for my son, Wishee Washee. Have you seen him? (*Yes.*) Have you? (*Yes!*) Well, I wish I had — he's late with the Emperor's washing. That's Aladdin's job really. My other son — but he's got so lazy lately. Just like his poor late father — Lanky Twankey. We called him Lanky because he was always making up tall stories. A model husband he was — not a working model, you understand. Well, he was superstitious, wasn't he: he wouldn't do any work in a week that had a Wednesday in it. When he died he left me dissolute. So now I run the Laundry. Which reminds me — my laundry list. (*She gets out her list and discovers it's a list of parties, birthdays, etc. This list is optional.*) Now, where was I . . . Oh yes: times are very hard. Aladdin's no use — always mooning about after some girl. And Wishee — well, he tries hard, but I don't know how we're going to manage. We can't pay the rent, and that horrid old Emperor Foo Wiff Pong says he's going to close down my Laundry. That'll cause a stink, I can tell you. But where there's life there's soap, I always say. And I like to dream of what I'll do when I'm rich . . .

Song: When I'm Rich (TWANKEY)

TWANKEY	WHEN I LOOK IN THE MIRROR AND SEE MYSELF OLD AND WORN AND GREY. WHEN I LOOK AT MY FACE I THINK "WHAT A DISGRACE!" THE LINES GET DEEPER EACH DAY.

I IMAGINE THE TIME WHEN I HAVEN'T A CARE,
NOT A TROUBLE TO CLOUD MY DAY.
NOW ISN'T IT FUNNY,
IT'S DREAMING OF MONEY
THAT DRIVES ALL MY WORRIES AWAY.

WHEN I'M RICH I'LL HAVE CASH —
I SHALL DRESS WITH STYLE AND PANACHE.
I SHALL LIVE IN A PALACE
THAT'S STRAIGHT OUT OF DALLAS,
AND MARRY A MAN WITH A 'TACHE.
I'LL BE GLAM, I'LL BE CHIC —
SHOP IN HARROD'S EACH DAY OF THE WEEK.
THERE ARE MANY THINGS WORSE
THAN A BOTTOMLESS PURSE,
WHEN I'M RICH, WHEN I'M RICH, WHEN I'M RICH!

WHEN I'M RICH I'LL BE FREE —
SPEND MY WEEKENDS AT CLACTON-ON-SEA.
TRAVEL ROUND IN A ROLLS
AS WE WAVE AT THE PROLES,
ALADDIN AND WISHEE AND ME.
AND THEN AFTER MY AFTERNOON REST,
AND LOOKING MY RAVISHING BEST,
I'LL GO DOWN TO THE GREEN
AND TAKE TEA WITH THE QUEEN,
WHEN I'M RICH, WHEN I'M RICH, WHEN I'M RICH!

I'LL BE PROUD, I'LL BE GRAND —
THEY'LL BOW AS I WALK DOWN THE STRAND.
WITH NO WORK TO BE DONE
I SHALL LIE IN THE SUN —
I'LL BE SECOND TO NONE —
I SHALL HAVE SO MUCH FUN,
WHEN I'M RICH, WHEN I'M RICH, WHEN I'M RICH!

(*Enter* WISHEE, *with basket* — ALADDIN *is hidden inside.*)

WISHEE	Watcha Kids!
AUDIENCE	Watcha Wishee!
TWANKEY	There you are, Wishee. You took your time.
WISHEE	Sorry, Mum. The Emperor's laundry weighs a ton this week.
TWANKEY	Good — we'll charge him double.

(*Enter* PING PONG, *blowing whistle.*)

PING PONG Clear the streets! Don't panic! Clear the streets! Make way for His Excellency Foo Wiff Pong — Emperor of Peking.

(*Enter all, including children, merchants and customers. Fanfare. Enter* EMPEROR. *All bow.*)

TWANKEY (*fanning herself*) Coo! Sniff that pong! How smelly he is!

EMPEROR I beg your pardon?

TWANKEY I said Foo Wiff Pong — your Excellentness!

EMPEROR Ping Pong. Read the Proclamation.

PING PONG Yes, your Pooiness. (*Slowly.*) I, Foo Wiff Pong, hereby proclaim —

EMPEROR Not like that, you dope. At the double.

PING PONG Double? Certainly, your Ponginess. (*Reads.*) I I Foo Foo Wiff Wiff Pong Pong hereby hereby proclaim proclaim —

EMPEROR What are you doing, you fool?

PING PONG I'm reading at the double double you fool fool.

EMPEROR Doh!

(EMPEROR *takes the proclamation and reads.*)

I, Foo Wiff Pong, hereby proclaim that owing to the precarious predicament of the Imperial Exchequer —

PING PONG (*aside*) He's run out of money.

EMPEROR All sabbaticals are hereby abolished —

PING PONG (*aside*) No more holidays.

ALL Boo!

EMPEROR But all operational inactivity is hereby alleviated.

PING PONG (*aside*) Everyone can have a job!

ALL	Hurrah!
EMPEROR	In exchange for zero-rated emoluments.
PING PONG	(*aside*) But no wages!
ALL	Boo!
EMPEROR	And the next person to go "Boo!" will go to prison — so there!
TWANKEY	Boo!
EMPEROR	Who was that?
TWANKEY	Boo . . . hoo, hoo, hoo! I was just crying, your Povertystrickenness: I'm so upset that you've run out of money. Boo —
ALL	Hoo, hoo, hoo!
EMPEROR	Silence! My daughter, Princess So-Shy, is coming through the gardens in a minute on her way to the Bath House. Remember: nobody is to look at her on pain of death! So — scram!
PING PONG	Clear the streets! Clear the streets! Don't panic! Clear the streets!

(PING PONG *chases everybody off.* EMPEROR *remains.* WISHEE *returns immediately to get the laundry basket.*)

WISHEE	Watcha Kids!
AUDIENCE	Watcha Wishee!

(WISHEE *falls over, as he does when audience respond loudly.*)

EMPEROR	What are you doing down there?
WISHEE	Getting up!
EMPEROR	What do you want?
WISHEE	Your smelly, your Washingship!
EMPEROR	What?

WISHEE	I mean your washing, your Smelliship!
EMPEROR	What?!
WISHEE	Your washing. Your washing.
EMPEROR	*I'm* not washing. I don't believe in it. My daughter's washing.
WISHEE	Hers as well.
EMPEROR	If you don't want your head chopped off, you'd better get moving. Chop chop.
WISHEE	Chop chop?
EMPEROR	(*axe mime*) Chop! Chop!
WISHEE	Aaarrrhhhh!!

(*Exit* WISHEE, *pursued by* EMPEROR. *Enter* SING SONG, *followed by* PRINCESS.)

SING SONG	Come on, Princess. The coast's clear.
PRINCESS	Worst luck! I tell you, Sing Song, I'm sick to death of being on my own all the time. It's so boring!
SING SONG	It would drive me round the bend.
PRINCESS	Maybe when I get married . . .
SING SONG	Don't think of getting married yet, Princess. Besides, I bet your father will choose you a rotten husband. You want to see the world first, and make your own choice.

(ALADDIN *opens the lid of the basket and sticks his head out.*)

ALADDIN	Hear, hear!

(*They turn and the* PRINCESS *screams.* ALADDIN *shuts the lid smartly.*)

PRINCESS	(*impressed*) What was that, Sing Song?
SING SONG	A boy, Princess.

PRINCESS   I didn't think boys were as nice-looking as that! Tell him to come out.

                   (SING SONG *flips open the lid of the basket.*)

SING SONG   You! Out!

                   (ALADDIN *gets out. He is transfixed by the* PRINCESS.)

PRINCESS   What's your name?

ALADDIN   Aladdin, Princess. I had to see you.

PRINCESS   And risk your life?

ALADDIN   I couldn't help it. I . . . I . . . (*He kneels.*) May I offer myself as your servant, Princess?

PRINCESS   You can't, Aladdin. If my father finds you here —

                   (*A whistle, off.*)

PRINCESS   Run for your life!

PING PONG   (*off*) Clear the streets!

PRINCESS   Run!

PING PONG   (*off*) Clear the streets!

ALADDIN   (*bowing*) Princess!

                   (ALADDIN *runs the wrong way and meets* PING PONG *entering.*)

PING PONG   Thief! Thief! Stop thief!

                   (ALADDIN *turns and* PING PONG *chases him across the stage brandishing his truncheon. Enter* EMPEROR *from the other side.*)

EMPEROR   What's going on?

                   (ALADDIN *stops short of bumping into the* EMPEROR *and ducks out of the way.*)

PING PONG   Don't panic! Don't panic!

	(EMPEROR *and* PING PONG *bump into each other and* ALADDIN *jumps back into the basket.*)
PING PONG	I've caught the thief, your Emperorship!
EMPEROR	You've caught me, you fool!
PING PONG	Sorry, your Rulership!
EMPEROR	Which way did he go, So-Shy?
PRINCESS	I don't know, father.
EMPEROR	Sing Song?
	(SING SONG *doesn't answer.*)
EMPEROR	(*crossly*) Sing Song!
	(PING PONG *starts singing.*)
EMPEROR	What are you doing, Ping Pong?
PING PONG	You say sing song. I sing song.
EMPEROR	Doh! Was that Aladdin?
PING PONG	Yes, your Dictatorship.
EMPEROR	Off with his head!
PRINCESS	No, father . . .
EMPEROR	Off with his head!

Song: Off With His Head (EMPEROR, PING PONG, SING SONG *and* PRINCESS)

EMPEROR

ALADDIN'S HAD THE NERVE TO FLOUT
PEKING'S SACRED LAW.
THE INSOLENCE OF THIS YOUNG LOUT
HAS SHOWN A FATAL FLAW.
AND IF HE THINKS THAT HE'LL ESCAPE,
WELL, I'VE GOT NEWS, MY SON.
FOR MY DESIRE TO SHOW MY IRE
HAS ONLY JUST BEGUN!

OFF WITH HIS HEAD!
OFF WITH HIS HEAD!
I WANT THAT BOY . . . DEAD!
CUT OFF HIS ARMS!

BOIL UP HIS BRAINS!
AND FLUSH ALL THE HORRIBLE BITS DOWN THE
　　　　　　　　　　　　　　　　　　　DRAINS!
OFF WITH HIS HEAD!

PRINCESS　　I BEG YOU FATHER, ON MY KNEES —
　　　　　　HAVE MERCY ON HIS SOUL.
　　　　　　YOU WANT TO CHOP HIM UP, BUT PLEASE
　　　　　　I'D RATHER HAVE HIM WHOLE!
　　　　　　HE DIDN'T MEAN TO BREAK THE LAW —
　　　　　　ALADDIN'S NOT THAT BAD.
　　　　　　HE'LL SAY HE'S SORRY, DAD, I'M SURE.
　　　　　　I THINK YOU'RE GOING MAD!

EMPEROR　}　OFF WITH HIS HEAD!
PING PONG　 OFF WITH HIS HEAD!
　　　　　　I WANT THAT BOY . . . DEAD!
　　　　　　PULL OUT HIS NAILS!
　　　　　　CHOP OFF HIS TOES!
　　　　　　FINGERS AND LEGS, EARS AND EYES AND NOSE!
　　　　　　OFF WITH HIS HEAD . . .

(EMPEROR *and* PING PONG *continue under the following.*)

PRINCESS　}　OH FATHER DEAR, YOU CANNOT MEAN
SING SONG　 TO BE SO AWFULLY CRUEL.
　　　　　　YOU'RE USUALLY SO KIND AND SWEET
　　　　　　AND, AS A RULE,
　　　　　　YOU'D NEVER HARM A POOR YOUNG LAD —
　　　　　　IT'S DREADFUL HOW YOU'VE CHANGED.
　　　　　　YOU USED TO BE MY DEAR OLD DAD,
　　　　　　BUT NOW YOU'RE QUITE DERANGED!

(ALADDIN *has come out of the basket. At the end of the song he manages, with the help of* SING SONG *and the* PRINCESS, *to push the* EMPEROR *and* PING PONG *into the basket and make his escape. Frontcloth in.*)

Scene Two

Frontcloth (B): Araby.

Flash. Enter ABANAZAR.

ABANAZAR　　Abanazar is my name —
　　　　　　Power absolute my aim.
　　　　　　You've travelled, courtesy of me,

From China here to Araby.
Don't be deceived — I hate you all.
You'll see me rise: I'll watch you fall!
It's boys and girls I most despise —
For picking noses, telling lies.
Little ones I like, of course:
Grilled, on toast, with lots of sauce!
Now to my plot: I have a scheme,
Following a recent dream.
I clearly saw, and thus it was foretold,
The world in Abanazar's stranglehold.
My power resided in a Magic Lamp —
Deep down inside a Cave . . . then, I got cramp!
Curses! Just as I was getting close, I woke:
My vision vanished in a puff of smoke.
Now, in despair, I rail and rant and rave:
Where is the Magic Lamp? And where the Cave?
I'll conjure up the Genie of the Ring:
She's rather slow, but she knows everything.
I rub the ring — command that you appear!
Come forth — thou 'thing' — come forth.

(*Flash. Enter* GENIE OF THE RING.)

GENIE   Hello, my dear!
At last! That ring! No fun cooped up in there:
Six hundred years, without a breath of air!
Me poor old legs — oh, and another thing —
I'm dying for a wee . . .

ABANAZAR   Just stop this wittering.
Tell me: where is the Lamp of which I dreamt last night?
I'm Master of the Ring, so — Genie — speak!

GENIE   Alright,
Keep your hair on! A Lamp? Now, let me see —
What kind of Lamp, exactly, might that be?
Neon, gas, or electricity, my dear?
An Anglepoise? A Miner's Lamp? A Chandelier?

ABANAZAR   A Magic Lamp, you fool — it *must* exist.

GENIE   Alright — don't get your knickers in a twist!
There *is* a Lamp — I cannot tell a lie —
Invisible to any passer-by.
Deep in a Cave it lies —

ABANAZAR   Be more precise!

GENIE	Stop shouting, dear — it isn't very nice.
ABANAZAR	Where is this Cave?
GENIE	In China, miles away. The journey takes forever and a day. The Cave is dismal, dark, and very damp — Haunted, too, I'm told . . .
ABANAZAR	Fetch me the Lamp!
GENIE	I can't, 'cos I'm immortal. There's a ban On spirits fetching lamps.
ABANAZAR	Then I'm your man!
GENIE	No!
ABANAZAR	Why not?
GENIE	Only a boy, who can tell no lie May fetch this Lamp.
ABANAZAR	I'll find one!
GENIE	You can try.
ABANAZAR	You know him, don't you — one that fits the bill?
GENIE	I might —
ABANAZAR	You do!
GENIE	Perhaps you're right!
ABANAZAR	I'd kill To have his name. Come on! You have to tell: Who is he? Where's he live?
GENIE	Oh, very well. A-lad-in Peking you should seek. My meaning's plain.
ABANAZAR	His name?
GENIE	Already told you!
ABANAZAR	Say again!

GENIE	A-lad-in Peking you should seek — alright?
ABANAZAR	His name, you fool! I can't wait here all night!
GENIE	I've said!
ABANAZAR	The boy — who is he?
GENIE	Mum's the word! I've told you twice.
ABANAZAR	Oh, this is quite absurd! What's he look like?
GENIE	Dark hair — slim and lanky.
ABANAZAR	What's his mother called?
GENIE	His Mum's name? Widow Twankey. She runs the Laundry.
ABANAZAR	Now I'll find the boy. He'll fetch the Lamp. I'll rule the world. What joy!
GENIE	Your fortune, Abanazar, will be brief. Disaster I foresee: you'll come to grief.
ABANAZAR	You've served your purpose. Fly me to Peking. And when you've done that: back into your ring!
GENIE	You want to fly? All right, I'll have a go: Turn once, turn twice, turn three times: Cheerio!

(*Exit both. Frontcloth out.*)

Scene Three

WIDOW TWANKEY'S *Laundry.*

Heath Robinson appearance: all vents and pipes and flues, strings and pulleys, soap suds, steam, etc. Rows and rows of washing to dry all over. Very cluttered and chaotic. Most can be painted, but "practical" essentials as follows: clothes line with TWANKEY'S *clothes (including bloomers, nighties, bras, etc — all spotted and patched and highly colourful) plus spare* PING PONG *uniform in prominent position. Antediluvian washing machine (though on modern design) and a huge* mangle (*big pads:* WISHEE *to go through*). *Ironing board leaning against wall with "out of order" sign. Other non-functional clutter as desired. Double swing doors.*

TWANKEY *discovered with small basket of washing.*

TWANKEY Oh, hello, dears, and welcome to my Laundry. Excuse my personals, won't you — but we don't stand on celebrities here. I was just hanging up my smalls and . . . (*Huge pair.*) . . . my bigs. And this I call my Big Ben bra: keeps me abreast of the times. (*Huge sneeze.*) Sorry, dears, I've got one of my dreadful sneezing attacks. Aladdin's always on at me to use a hanky, but I never seem to remember. Tell you what — will you remind me if I forget? (*Yes.*)

(*She teaches "Hanky Twankey" routine.*)

Thank you, dears. You may wonder what a woman of culture and intoxication like me is doing running a Laundry. Well, after my old man pegged out, I began to take in washing — just to rub along, you understand. So I put a card in the newsagent's window: "Respectable Young Widow Wants Washing." I got some funny replies, I can tell you!

(*Enter* WISHEE *and Children with the Palace laundry basket.*)

WISHEE Watcha Kids!

AUDIENCE Watcha Wishee!

WISHEE Watcha Mum!

(TWANKEY *sneezes.*)

AUDIENCE Hanky, Twankey!

TWANKEY Thank you, dears.

WISHEE Here's the washing, Mum.

(*She opens the basket. Two of the smallest children jump out.*)

TWANKEY Get out of there, you laundry layabouts! Is that all? Business is terrible. I blame the repression.

WISHEE	Cheer up, Mum. You should advertise.
TWANKEY	Advertise?
WISHEE	Yes. Listen, we'll show you.

Song: Trot Down to Twankey's Laundry (WISHEE — TWANKEY *and Children join where appropriate*.)

WISHEE
WHEN WASHDAY'S APPROACHING,
YOUR SHIRTS ARE ALL GREY —
AND YOUR SOCKS HAVE WALKED OUT ON THEIR OWN;
AND YOU NOTICE A LITTLE BIT MORE EVERY DAY
JUST HOW MUCH THE MOULD ON YOUR HANKY
                                      HAS GROWN.

WHEN YOU'VE RUN OUT OF UNDIES
BY SATURDAY NIGHT —
AND YOUR BEST FRIEND HAS WHISPERED "B.O." —
PUT THE FUN BACK IN MONDAYS,
BE WHITER THAN WHITE —
THERE'S ONLY ONE PLACE FOR YOUR WASHING TO GO.

JUST TROT DOWN TO TWANKEY'S LAUNDRY —
SHE CAN TAKE YOUR BAD RAGS,
TURN THEM INTO GLAD RAGS.
TROT DOWN TO TWANKEY'S LAUNDRY,
AND WASH YOUR WASHDAY BLUES AWAY.

IF YOUR MAC IS IN A MANGLE —
T-SHIRTS IN A TANGLE
AND YOUR PANTS ARE PAST THEIR SELL-BY DATE.
YOUR NIGHTIE'S IN A STEW,
YOUR WHITES ARE LOOKING BLUE
AND YOUR TIGHTS ARE IN A TERRIBLE STATE.

JUST TROT DOWN TO TWANKEY'S LAUNDRY —
NOBODY CAN BEAT HER,
HAVE YOU SMELLING SWEETER.
TROT DOWN TO TWANKEY'S LAUNDRY,
AND WASH THOSE WASHDAY BLUES AWAY!

(*Advertising spiel as follows, underscored.*)

WISHEE	We took this pair . . . (*Child 1 holds up ordinary pair.*) . . . of my Mum's best bloomers —

TWANKEY	Wishee!
WISHEE	And washed them in new improved Twanko Micro. The result — (*Child 2 holds up tiny replica pair.*)
TWANKEY	A little miracle! We then washed the same pair —
WISHEE	In Twanko Maxi. The result — (*Child 3 holds up huge replica pair.*)
TWANKEY	A bigger miracle! We then washed the same pair —
WISHEE	In Twanko Colour. The result — (*Child 4 holds up another huge pair, but changed colour.*)
TWANKEY	A blooming miracle!
WISHEE	So, if you want your whites whiter, your coloureds brighter, and your tights tighter, use new, improved —
	(*Children reverse the garments they are still holding up, on which is written in large capitals: "Twanko".*)
ALL	TWANKO!
WISHEE	IF YOUR DRESS IS IN A MESS — YOUR VEST IS PAST ITS BEST, AND YOUR KIMONO'S STARTING TO DECOMPOSE. YOUR KNICKERS AND YOUR BOXERS ARE SMELLY AND OBNOXIOUS, AND EVEN THE DOG'S BEEN HOLDING HIS NOSE! WE'LL TAKE THEM ALL AWAY — RETURN THEM IN A DAY: AND HAVE YOU SMELLING AS SWEET AS A ROSE.
ALL	SO TROT DOWN TO TWANKEY'S LAUNDRY — WE CAN TAKE YOUR BAD RAGS, TURN THEM INTO GLAD RAGS. TROT DOWN TO TWANKEY'S LAUNDRY, AND WASH YOUR WASHDAY BLUES AWAY —
WISHEE	(HEAR WHAT WE SAY?)
ALL	AND WASH YOUR WASHDAY BLUES AWAY!
TWANKEY	Well, thank you, dears. You've really cheered me up. Now let's get down to some hard work.

CHILDREN	'Bye, Widow Twankey! 'Bye!
	(*Exit Children.*)
TWANKEY	Well, what a washout, Wishee. Now have you seen that idle, good-for-nothing brother of yours?
WISHEE	Not recently, Mum. Don't worry, I'll help you with the washing.
	(*He takes the* EMPEROR'S *washing out of the basket and scatters it about.*)
TWANKEY	No, Wishee. You don't know how the machines work.
WISHEE	You can teach me, Mum. (*Pleading.*) Please!
TWANKEY	Alright, but if you're going to help me you must do *exactly* what I say.
WISHEE	Exactly what you say. Right.
TWANKEY	First we load the washing machine. So — open the door.
WISHEE	Open the door. Right.
	(*He opens the door of the laundry.*)
TWANKEY	No, Wishee. We've got to put the washing inside the machine.
WISHEE	(*not hearing*) What?
TWANKEY	*Inside* the machine, Wishee.
WISHEE	Inside the machine. Right.
	(WISHEE *gets into the washing machine.*)
TWANKEY	Where's Wishee?
AUDIENCE	Inside the machine. (*Etc.*)
	(TWANKEY *opens the machine door.*)
WISHEE	Can I come out now, Mum?

TWANKEY	Get out of there, Wishee. That is a very dangerous thing to do. Now — what do we put in the washing machine, Wishee?
WISHEE	Washing, Mum.

(*He does so.*)

TWANKEY	Now — shut the door.
WISHEE	Shut the door —

(WISHEE *makes for the main door, then turns back knowingly.*)

Aha!

(WISHEE *shuts the machine.*)

TWANKEY	Now, put in the soap.
WISHEE	Put in the soap. Right.

(WISHEE *takes a huge slab of soap and chucks it in.*)

TWANKEY	And turn on the machine.
WISHEE	(*incredulous*) Turn? On the machine? Really?
TWANKEY	Yes — *turn* on the machine.
WISHEE	If you say so!

(WISHEE *climbs on top of the machine and starts turning round.*)

TWANKEY	No, no, no, you stupid boy! Stop! Turn on . . . I'll do it.

(TWANKEY *bangs the machine, which vibrates loudly and violently, and* WISHEE *with it.*)

WISHEE	Can I get down, please, Mum?
TWANKEY	Yes, yes, yes.

(WISHEE *jumps off, and continues to judder until* TWANKEY *bangs on the machine again, and both stop.*)

TWANKEY	Now I'll show you how to use the mangle.
WISHEE	The mangle. Right.
TWANKEY	Take that wet nightshirt.
WISHEE	Right.
TWANKEY	And put it through the mangle as I turn the handle.

(*She starts turning the handle.*)

WISHEE	Put it through the mangle . . .

(*He puts the cloth in and follows it through the mangle.*)

. . . as you turn the aaaarrrrhhhhh!

TWANKEY	Wishee! Are you alright?

(*She turns the handle the other way and cardboard/flat WISHEE comes through.*)

WISHEE	(*off*) Don't worry, Mum. I'm just feeling a little bored.
TWANKEY	Then go and have a lie down. You'll soon come round.

(TWANKEY *throws off the board. Enter* ALADDIN.)

ALADDIN	Hi, Ma!
TWANKEY	Aladdin — there you are. I'm very cross with you. You're a lazy, idle, good-for-nothing . . . dear . . . delightful boy. (*She gives him a big hug.*) Where have you been?
ALADDIN	Escaping from the Emperor, Ma.
TWANKEY	Why? What have you done?
ALADDIN	I cannot tell a lie, Ma. I had a little peek.
TWANKEY	A little peek?
ALADDIN	Yes, Ma.
TWANKEY	I'm having no dogs in my Laundry.
ALADDIN	No, Ma. I had a peek at the Princess.

TWANKEY	But you know the law in Peking.
ALADDIN	Yes, Ma.
TWANKEY	No peeking.
ALADDIN	No, Ma.
TWANKEY	You'll be the death of me.
ALADDIN	I'll be the death of me, Ma. The Emperor's going to have my head chopped off.
TWANKEY	Over my dead body.
ALADDIN	Yes — that too!

(*Enter* WISHEE.)

WISHEE	Watcha Kids!
AUDIENCE	Watcha Wishee!
ALADDIN	Where have you been, Wishee?
WISHEE	I had a rather pressing engagement.

(*Three knocks at the door.*)

ALL	The Emperor!
TWANKEY	Into the basket! Quick!

(WISHEE *opens the basket.* ALADDIN *jumps in.*)

TWANKEY	Do come in, your Worthlessness.

(*Enter* SING SONG.)

SING SONG	Widow Twankey —
TWANKEY	Oh, it's you dear.
SING SONG	The Emperor's looking for Aladdin.
TWANKEY	Don't worry, dear. We've hidden him.

SING SONG	In that basket?
TWANKEY	How did you guess?
SING SONG	They're bound to look there. It's obvious.
WISHEE	He needs a disguise.
SING SONG	Brilliant!
TWANKEY	Anybody got any ideas?
SING SONG	What about Ping Pong's spare uniform?
WISHEE	Brilliant!
SING SONG	(*helping* ALADDIN *put it on*) Come on, Aladdin — put it on. Now you'll be the safest person in Peking, because you'll be looking for yourself!
	(*Three knocks.*)
ALL	The Emperor!
PING PONG	(*off*) Open up in the name Foo Wiff Pong, the very high Emperor of Peking.
SING SONG	Quick! Hide! And don't come out till I give the password.
ALADDIN	The password. Right. (*He makes to go and returns.*) What's the password?
SING SONG	Er . . . er . . . "Gillette."
ALADDIN	"Gillette" — right. (*He hides.*)
TWANKEY	Why "Gillette"?
SING SONG	Because it's a close shave.
	(*Three more knocks.*)
ALL	The Emperor!
	(SING SONG *and* WISHEE *sit on the basket.*)
PING PONG	(*off*) I'm going to break this door down!

TWANKEY	Alright . . .
PING PONG	One!
TWANKEY	. . . Keep your pigtail on!
PING PONG	Two!
TWANKEY	I'm coming.
	(TWANKEY *opens the door just as* PING PONG *has taken a run at it.*)
PING PONG	Three!
	(*Enter* PING PONG *at a run. Trip and pratfall.* EMPEROR *follows sedately.*)
TWANKEY	(*forced jollity*) Welcome, your Warship! Excuse the chaos, won't you.
EMPEROR	Widow Twankey —
TWANKEY	Always in high spirits here.
EMPEROR	Widow Twankey —
TWANKEY	Well, high on spirits, anyway.
EMPEROR	We've come for Aladdin.
TWANKEY	He's left.
EMPEROR	Left?
TWANKEY	That's right! Left!
EMPEROR	Right! Did you hear that, Ping Pong? He's left.
PING PONG	Left?
EMPEROR	Right. Left.
PING PONG	Right. Left . . . Right, left, right . . .
	(PING PONG *starts marching.* EMPEROR *cuffs him.*)
EMPEROR	Doh! Search every nook and cranny.

WISHEE	I'm not a crook!
TWANKEY	And I'm not a nanny!
EMPEROR	I know Aladdin's here somewhere.
TWANKEY	You surely don't think he's in that laundry basket, do you, your Flagship?
EMPEROR	(*getting the idea*) Aha!
WISHEE	(*guilty*) He's not!
SING SONG	(*guilty*) We promise!
EMPEROR	Ping Pong. Open the basket.
WISHEE SING SONG }	Oh, no!

(*Drumroll.* PING PONG *flings back the lid.*)

PING PONG	He's not here, Wiffy-Pooh!
EMPEROR	What!
PING PONG	I mean Foohy-Wiff!
EMPEROR	Search right down to the bottom. He must be there.
TWANKEY	(*distracting attention*) I've got something important to tell you, your Battleship.
EMPEROR	What's that?
TWANKEY	Jack and Jill Came down the hill — Both were quite upset. There'd been a theft — One Rolo left: Jack went without — Gillette!

(SING SONG *and* WISHEE *join loudly on* "Gillette", *and at same time tip* PING PONG *into the basket.* ALADDIN, *dressed as* PING PONG, *appears instantly and shuts the lid.*)

EMPEROR	Well, Ping Pong?

ALADDIN	Definitely not in the basket, Emperor.
SING SONG	Come on, Wishee — let's take this washing back to the Palace.
WISHEE	'Bye, everyone!

(*They wheel basket off quickly, nearly knocking over the* EMPEROR.)

EMPEROR	Doh!
ALADDIN	Oh, most wise and wonderful Foo Wiff Pong — why don't I go and warn the Princess that Aladdin's on the loose?
EMPEROR	Sensible suggestion, Ping Pong. Maybe I won't cut your wages after all.
ALADDIN	Thank you very much, your most excellent Excellency. (*Slapping him on the back.*) Toodle-pip!

(*Exit* ALADDIN.)

EMPEROR	Doh!

(TWANKEY *laughs*.)

EMPEROR	And as for you, you wretched, wrinkled, wittering washer-women — I'm warning you. Pay your rent within three days or I shall close down this antediluvian doss-house of a wash-house.

(PING PONG *bursts in, very out of breath*.)

PING PONG	Pong . . . Wong . . . Fong Poo Wiff . . .
EMPEROR	What now?
PING PONG	Aladdin wasn't in the basket.
EMPEROR	You just told me that, you fool.
PING PONG	What?
EMPEROR	Did you find the Princess?
PING PONG	No — why?

EMPEROR	You said you'd go and warn her.
PING PONG	When?
EMPEROR	Just now.
PING PONG	I didn't.
EMPEROR	You did.
PING PONG	Didn't!
EMPEROR	Did!
PING PONG	Didn't!
EMPEROR	Did!
PING PONG	Didn't!!
EMPEROR	DID SO!!
	(*Pause.*)
TWANKEY	(*quietly*) Didn't.
PING PONG	See!
EMPEROR	Right. That does it. I am cutting your wages. Now get out!
PING PONG	Cutting my wages, but —
EMPEROR	Out! Out! Out!
	(EMPEROR *boots him out.*)
EMPEROR	And as for your delinquent son Aladdin — the peeping Tom of Peking — he'll be a foot shorter by the time I've finished with him. Oooh, I do love a good execution. Good day!
	(*Exit* EMPEROR.)
TWANKEY	Good riddance! Oh — everything's gone wrong. I've got no money, no friends, and Aladdin's going to have his head chopped off. Whatever shall I do?
	(*She cries, then sneezes.*)

AUDIENCE   Hanky, Twankey!

TWANKEY   Thank you, dears.

(*Enter* ABANAZAR.)

ABANAZAR   Excuse me!

TWANKEY   Who are you?

ABANAZAR   I didn't knock.
Just passing by — heard crying — quite a shock!

TWANKEY   What's that to you?

ABANAZAR   Here — borrow my hanky.
I'm looking for a widow — name of Twankey.
Wise, I'm told, and kind — but very poor.

TWANKEY   Who said?

ABANAZAR   I'm her long-lost brother-in-law:
Abanazar.

TWANKEY   My husband never said
He had a brother. Anyway — he's dead.
How do I know you're telling me the truth?

ABANAZAR   Me?

TWANKEY   Yes!

ABANAZAR   Deceive a women of your youth
And beauty?

TWANKEY   Ooooh . . . !

ABANAZAR   Let me prove I'm sincere:
This is for you.

TWANKEY   A diamond necklace!

ABANAZAR   Here:
Take it. It's yours. I'm a man of some wealth.

TWANKEY   Sorry! I wasn't feeling quite myself
Just now. Goes to show: you never can tell!

ALADDIN

	I didn't know my in-laws very well.
ABANAZAR	Trust me now?
TWANKEY	Oh, yes!
ABANAZAR	(*aside*) The fool! (*To her.*) You have a son, I understand. He cannot tell a lie?
TWANKEY	That's right, I have. His name's Aladdin. Why?
ABANAZAR	(*aside*) Of course! "A-lad-in Peking you should seek," The Genie said. (*To her.*) Where can I find him? Speak!
TWANKEY	He's dressed as a policeman, with a funny hat. Just ask for Ping Pong: he'll answer to that.
ABANAZAR	I'm much obliged. It's been a great pleasure.
TWANKEY	The pleasure's mine! (*Aside.*) Isn't he a treasure!
ABANAZAR	I must be off!
TWANKEY	Away so soon?
ABANAZAR	'Fraid so.
TWANKEY	You'll have a cup of tea before you go? (*Aside.*) Sexy *and* rich: must he my lucky day! (*To him.*) The kettle's boiled. Stay there. Don't go away!
	(*Exit* TWANKEY.)
ABANAZAR	Fell clean into my trap! At last! I'll get the lamp — the die is cast. As for the lad who cannot tell a lie: I'll leave him in the Cave — to DIE!
	(*Frontcloth in.*)

Scene Four

Frontcloth (A): Street in Peking.

Enter PING PONG *and* ALADDIN (*dressed as* PING PONG) *from opposite directions: quickly, but deep in thought. As they reach centre, both stop abruptly when faced with each other.*

BOTH Aaah!

PING PONG (*to audience*) That was lucky. I nearly walked into that mirror!

(PING PONG *gets out his comb to do his hair in the mirror or polishes his specs, or other simple activity.* ALADDIN *has time to copy the action.*)

PING PONG (*to audience*) I'm really fed up. Foo Wiff Pong tells me I told him something I never told him, and then tells me off for telling him I never told him what he says I told him — and now he's cutting my wages for not doing what I've told him I never said I'd do in the first place.

ALADDIN What?

PING PONG (*turning in*) What?

ALADDIN Nothing!

(PING PONG *turns out again and double-takes.* ALADDIN *copies series of double takes that* PING PONG *tries out in the mirror. Increasingly complex and comic actions — perhaps disco dancing — till* PING PONG *is satisfied that nothing is amiss.*)

PING PONG Well, I can't hang around talking to you lot. I've got to find Aladdin. See ya!

ALADDIN See ya!

(*Both turn and go.* PING PONG *clocks* ALADDIN'S *reply just before exiting. He turns and sees* ALADDIN *exiting.*)

PING PONG Hey! You! Come back!

(*He runs back. As he reaches the centre again there is a loud "mirror-breaking" crash and he falls over holding his nose.*)

PING PONG Aaaarrrrhhhh!!

(*Enter* ABANAZAR.)

ABANAZAR It's him! Aladdin! Just as Twankey said.
Dressed as a policeman — helmet on his head.

	She called him Ping Pong — nickname, I suppose. What's happened?
PING PONG	I'm in pain! I've hurt my nose Against this mirror!
ABANAZAR	(*aside*) Mad as a hatter! Still — provided I get the Lamp, no matter. (*To him.*) Ping Pong, isn't it?
PING PONG	Yes, that's right, that's me.
ABANAZAR	A man of fighting spirit, I can see. I have a little job I need to do. Fancy earning an extra yen or two?
PING PONG	How much?
ABANAZAR	What's your weekly wage?
PING PONG	Two yen, *but* After today that's likely to be cut.
ABANAZAR	Two measly yen a week? That's quite absurd! Two thousand yen I'll offer, on my word.
PING PONG	Two thousand yen!!
ABANAZAR	Per week! We leave in half an hour. Meet me back here.
PING PONG	You bet!

(*Exit* PING PONG.)

| ABANAZAR | Aladdin's in my power! It's all so simple — almost Heaven-sent! He's rather dim, but — |

(*Enter* ALADDIN *from opposite side*.)

| | Aaaahhh! I thought you went . . . Didn't you just . . . ? Surely there can't be two! Twins or what? |
| ALADDIN | What? Oh . . . us! How do you do? (*aside*) It's very trying being in disguise: It's *kind* of lying, without telling lies! |

ABANAZAR Are you Aladdin?

ALADDIN (*aside*) What am I to say?
Can't lie. I think I'll simply walk away.

ABANAZAR Answer my question!

ALADDIN Sorry: not today!
I'm needed at the Palace right away.

(*Exit* ALADDIN.)

ABANAZAR Curses! I'll have to call the Genie here.
She'll know. I rub my ring. Genie: appear!

(*Enter* GENIE OF THE RING.)

GENIE What now? I'd only just got off to sleep.
This job's enough to make you want to weep!

ABANAZAR I'd just found Aladdin, nicknamed Ping Pong,
When I met his double, his brother —

GENIE You're wrong!
He has got a brother — his name's Wishee.
You didn't meet him.

ABANAZAR You mean there are THREE?!

GENIE No, you're confused: Aladdin's in disguise.
You're very stupid not to realise.

ABANAZAR Fetch me Aladdin. Here. To this very spot.

GENIE Oh, if you insist. When?

ABANAZAR Now — on the dot.

GENIE I can't say I'm keen.

ABANAZAR What choice have you got?
You can't disobey — it's part of the plot!

GENIE Then I'll not fail you, Master.

ABANAZAR No. You'd better not!

(*Exit* ABANAZAR *and* GENIE OF THE RING. *Frontcloth out.*)

Scene Five.

The Palace Gardens.

PRINCESS *on small stool doing needlework and* SING SONG *sitting on the ground beside her.* ALADDIN (*still as* PING PONG) *parading up and down as guard. He can hear everything.*

PRINCESS	(*throwing down needlework*) I'm so bored, Sing Song. Nothing exciting ever happens . . . Except . . .
SING SONG	Except what?
PRINCESS	Yesterday. When Aladdin jumped out of that basket. Do you know, Sing Song, I lay awake all last night thinking about him.
SING SONG	Oh dear!
PRINCESS	Who is he, Sing Song? Is he a Prince?
SING SONG	Er . . . (*Catching* ALADDIN'S *eye.*) No!
PRINCESS	Then who is he?
SING SONG	You won't like this.
PRINCESS	Tell me, tell me, tell me!
SING SONG	Alright. His mother runs the launderette, he hasn't got a yen to his name, and his only recommendation is that he's marginally less dozy than his brother, Wishee Washee. Mind you, he's rather sweet.
PRINCESS	Who — Aladdin?
SING SONG	No — Wishee.
PRINCESS	Are you in love with Wishee?
SING SONG	No . . . well . . . no . . . of course not! I mean, he is nice. We're good mates, that's all.
PRINCESS	I'm in love with Aladdin.

(Aladdin *stops, almost swooning.*)

Sing Song You can't be!

Princess Yes, I can. Love at first sight. I've read about it in books. It's always happening to Princesses. Only they tend to go for Princes as a rule. I've fallen in love with a Laundry boy, and his name's Aladdin.

Sing Song Your father will never let you marry him.

Princess I shall marry whoever I choose.

Song: Far Away (Princess, Sing Song *and* Aladdin)

Princess
I AM TIRED OF A LIFE WHERE MY TIME IS NOT MY OWN,
AND MY DAYS ARE ORDERED AND BLEAK.
I CAN THINK WHAT I LIKE IN THE PRISON THAT'S MY HOME,
BUT THESE THOUGHTS I CAN NEVER SPEAK.

HOW I LONG FOR THE DAY
WHEN I CAN RUN AWAY,
ESCAPE FROM THE BARS OF THIS GILDED CAGE.
WATCH ME FLY —
OH SO HIGH!
IN THE BOOK OF MY LIFE IT'S TIME TO WRITE A BRAND NEW PAGE.

Sing Song (*spoken*) But Princess — your Highness — your subjects love you. They all admire and respect you!

Princess
I AM SICK OF A WORLD WHERE I MUST NOT BE SEEN,
WHERE THE PEOPLE TURN AWAY WHEN I PASS THEM BY.

Sing Song
BUT THEY ENVY YOU, YOUR HIGHNESS
THEY'RE ABSOLUTELY GREEN —
THEY'D LOVE TO LIVE YOUR LIFE —

Princess
WELL LET THEM TRY!
THEY CAN HAVE IT ALL —
I DON'T CARE HOW LOW I FALL.
I'D BE POOR BUT HAPPY, I KNOW.
FOR I'VE FOUND THE BOY
WHO'LL BRING ME JOY,

AND WHEREVER HE TRAVELS, I'LL GO!

FAR AWAY TO A LAND OF BEAUTY,
PLACE OF SIMPLE PLEASURES.
I'D GO TODAY IF HE'D GO WITH ME —
HE'D BE MY GREATEST TREASURE!

FAR AWAY TO A LAND OF SUNSHINE,
TAKE ME THERE — I'LL GO WITH YOU.
OH HAPPY DAY, IF HE'D BE MINE:
I'D BE FAITHFUL, HONEST, LOVING AND TRUE . . .

PRINCESS	FAR AWAY —
ALADDIN	TO A LAND OF BEAUTY —
SING SONG	PLACE OF SIMPLE PLEASURES.
ALADDIN	I'D GO TODAY IF SHE'D GO WITH ME —
PRINCESS } ALADDIN	HE'D BE MY GREATEST TREASURE! SHE'D BE MY GREATEST TREASURE!
SING SONG	FAR AWAY —
ALADDIN	TO A LAND OF SUNSHINE —
PRINCESS	TAKE ME THERE —
ALADDIN	I'LL GO WITH YOU.
SING SONG	OH HAPPY DAY,
PRINCESS } ALADDIN	IF HE'LL BE MINE — IF SHE'LL BE MINE —
PRINCESS	I'LL BE FAITHFUL.
ALADDIN	I'LL BE FAITHFUL.
PRINCESS	I'LL BE HONEST.
ALADDIN	I'LL BE HONEST.
ALL	HE'LL/I'LL BE FAITHFUL, HONEST, LOVING AND TRUE!

(*Enter* EMPEROR.)

EMPEROR Ping Pong! Ping Pong!

(ALADDIN *doesn't reply — lovestruck*.)

EMPEROR What's the matter with the man? (*Shouts*.) Ping Pong!

ALADDIN (*jumping*) Sorry, your Loveliness!

EMPEROR What!

ALADDIN	I mean — sorry, your Guv'nership!
EMPEROR	Go and fetch my latest Proclamation.
ALADDIN	Certainly, your Prettiness!
EMPEROR	What!
ALADDIN	I mean — your Princeliness!
EMPEROR	And hurry up!
ALADDIN	(*going, but still fixed on the* PRINCESS) Yes, your Gorgeousness!

(*Exit* ALADDIN.)

EMPEROR	Doh!
PRINCESS	What's this new Proclamation about, father?
EMPEROR	I've thought up this splendiferously clever new plan for making money.
SING SONG	Here we go.
EMPEROR	Shut your mouth! I'm going to offer you in marriage to the highest bidder. I get lots of dosh and you get a rich husband.
PRINCESS	I don't want a rich husband.
EMPEROR	Don't be silly.
SING SONG	She's going to marry Aladdin.
EMPEROR	Not that lazy, lanky, laundry lay-about, she's not. Don't make me laugh.

(*Enter* PING PONG.)

EMPEROR	Ah, Ping Pong. Come here — chop chop!
PING PONG	You speaking to me, sunshine?
EMPEROR	Eh?

PING PONG	'Cos if you are, matey, you'd better watch your P's and Q's.
EMPEROR	What!
PING PONG	Here's your rotten Proclamation.

(*He throws the proclamation across the stage.*)

EMPEROR	How dare you!
PING PONG	I dare, Pong-face, 'cos I've got another job, Wiff-bag. With real wages, Fooey-Poohey! I resign, get it? I quit! See ya, Princess! So long, Sing Song! And Pooh to you, Wiff Pong Foo!

(PING PONG *saunters out.*)

EMPEROR	Well really! I've never been so insulted in my life!
SING SONG	Don't get out much, then?
EMPEROR	(*apoplectic*) Wait till I get my hands on that fatuously flat-footed apology for a Peking policeman. I'll . . . I'll . . .

(*He passes out.*)

PRINCESS	Oh dear — he's passed out. (*She and* SING SONG *fan him.*) Don't get yourself in such a lather, father. (*He comes round.*)
SING SONG	Why don't you read that nice new Proclamation of yours, your Highness? That'll cheer you up.
EMPEROR	Good idea. Hear ye! Hear ye — you miserable, uncivilised citizens of Peking!

(*Enter children, merchants* (GENIE OF THE RING *and* SLAVE OF THE LAMP) *and* TWANKEY *and* WISHEE *in character.*)

I, Foo Wiff Pong, hereby proclaim that owing to the dismal condition of the Imperial Budget —

WISHEE	What did he say?
TWANKEY	He said his budgie's not very well.
EMPEROR	Budget, you fool. Budget.

(TWANKEY *moves away*.)

TWANKEY Alright, alright.

(*Enter* ALADDIN, *still dressed as* PING PONG, *unseen by* EMPEROR.)

EMPEROR I propose to give the hand of my sole heir — Princess So-Shy — to whomsoever shall offer the highest consideration.

TWANKEY He's going to sell off his daughter!

ALL Shame!

WISHEE To the highest bidder!

ALL Shame!

ALADDIN Whether she likes it or not!

ALL Shame!

EMPEROR Ping Pong!

ALADDIN I'm sorry, your Stateliness: I couldn't find your Proclamation anywhere.

EMPEROR (*ominously*) Come here!

ALADDIN (*innocently*) Certainly, your Exaltedness!

EMPEROR As a punishment for your scurrilous impertinence, I sentence you to thirty days in prison on cabbage and cod liver oil.

ALL Ugh!

EMPEROR And strip you of the office of Constable.

(*He strips off "Ping Pong's" uniform to reveal* ALADDIN.)

EMPEROR Aladdin!

ALL Aladdin!

EMPEROR Seize him!

ALADDIN

                    (*Chase, after which* ALADDIN *is seized by the two
                    merchants.* TWANKEY *starts to cry.*)

EMPEROR   (*spoken*) And as for you, you lamentably large liability of a
                laundry-lady, if you are not out of that dreary washeteria
                first thing tomorrow morning, I'll chop *your* head off, too.
                Oooh — I do love a good execution. Off with his head.

                    (*He throws* ALADDIN *down. Blackout. Frontcloth in.*)

                            Scene Six

Frontcloth (A): *Street in Peking.*

Enter ABANAZAR.

ABANAZAR   My plan is working brilliantly.
                I'll get the Lamp — you wait and see!

                    (*Enter* PING PONG, *dressed for safari. The more ridiculous
                    his travelling outfit the better: camping equipment,
                    rucksack, suitcases etc. Some element of his uniform must
                    still be prominent, for* ABANAZAR *to recognise him.*)

PING PONG   Hi, boss! It's me! Packed and ready to go!
                Ping Pong reporting — at your service! So —
                When are we off?

ABANAZAR   You're not Aladdin?

PING PONG   No —
                Ping Pong's the name — PC Ping Pong, in fact —
                Chief of Police to his Royal High —

ABANAZAR   You're sacked!

PING PONG   No — I resigned — quite voluntarily.
                I'd had enough of Foo Wiff Pong. You see
                To be frank — I mean, between you and me,
                He stank! To high Heaven! Yes, Siree!
                So when you offered me a job —

ABANAZAR   You're fired!

PING PONG   I have to say I was pleased to be hired.

ABANAZAR   Dismissed!

PING PONG	What? But . . . but my two thousand yen . . . You promised.
ABANAZAR	Out! I won't tell you again!
PING PONG	You nasty double-crossing rotter. (*Lost for words.*) Ooooh! You wait: Ping Pong will get even with you!

(*Exit* PING PONG *in disgust.*)

ABANAZAR	Where is that Genie of the Ring — she's late.

(*Enter* GENIE, *with* ALADDIN. ABANAZAR *doesn't see them.*)

GENIE	He's so impatient.
ABANAZAR	I can hardly wait To see the boy . . . Ah, there you are. About time, too.
GENIE	Alright, keep your hair on: what's got into you? Think yourself lucky I found Aladdin alive: He was having his head chopped off at half past five.
ALADDIN	What's that to him? Who is he anyway?
GENIE	I'll do the introductions, if I may. Abanazar — Aladdin. Aladdin — Abanazar.
ABANAZAR	Aladdin — I'm the long-lost brother of your father. We were separated in the bloom of youth.
ALADDIN	How do I know you're telling me the truth? You could be anyone for all I know.
ABANAZAR	Like to make some money?
ALADDIN	Yes . . . well . . . no!
ABANAZAR	How's this for starters?

(*He gives* ALADDIN *a bag of gold, marked "gold".*)

ALADDIN	What?
ABANAZAR	A bag of gold. Take it. It's yours.

GENIE	Aladdin —
ABANAZAR	I've been told You love the Princess.
ALADDIN	Who said?
ABANAZAR	So-Shy? So fair? The Emperor her father's in despair. He'll sell his daughter to the highest bidder. You're poor! You love her! Like to re-consider?
ALADDIN	But I could never be as rich as that —
ABANAZAR	You'll make a mint: if not, I'll eat my hat. Now listen carefully — don't breathe a sound: There's buried treasure hidden underground. Emeralds and diamonds — gems beyond compare — Overnight, my son, you'll be a millionaire!
ALADDIN	Hang on a minute: what's in this for you? And what is it that you want *me* to do?
ABANAZAR	Now that's exactly what I thought you'd ask. A Lamp I want — a very simple task. Rusty old thing — sentimental value.
ALADDIN	Just an old lamp?
ABANAZAR	Fetch it for me, will you?
ALADDIN	Why can't you get it?
ABANAZAR	I'm tall, and too fat. The entrance is tiny: simple as that!
ALADDIN	But —
ABANAZAR	Make up your mind. There's no time to lose. Poverty or riches: which do you choose?
ALADDIN	I'll do it.
ABANAZAR	Good lad: I knew you were brave. Genie of the Ring: fly us to the Cave!
GENIE	It's only three miles: quicker to walk.

ACT ONE

ABANAZAR   You're wicked and vile!

GENIE   You're one to talk!

ABANAZAR   Obey my command!

GENIE   Not on your nelly.
               I fancy a night in front of the telly.
               Good luck, Aladdin. Rather you than me.

               (*Exit* GENIE OF THE RING.)

ALADDIN   What did she mean by that?

ABANAZAR   You'll see!
               (*Aside*.) Now Aladdin is my slave!
               I get the Lamp — he finds his grave.
               I'll see you later at the Cave:
               Stop hissing will you — and behave!

               (*Exit* ABANAZAR *with* ALADDIN. *Frontcloth out*.)

Scene Seven

(A) *Outside the cave.*

A threatening rockface with cave entrance (sliding panel) "concealed" at bottom. The main scene (B) is set behind this rockface and will be revealed after ALADDIN *passes through the entrance. Another hidden entrance at the top will then open so that* ALADDIN *appears high up, to give the impression of a largely underground cave, into which* ALADDIN *will descend at beginning of (B).*

Atmosphere outside the cave is hauntingly sinister, but not quite as grim or forbidding as inside.

Short "ballet" of two three-headed Chinese Bogwoppits (played by children). They scatter as ABANAZAR'S *voice is heard.*

ABANAZAR   (*off*) Come on, boy!

               (*Enter* ABANAZAR, *followed by a reluctant* ALADDIN.)

ABANAZAR   Come on!

ALADDIN   I'm nervous, Uncle — that's the truth.

ABANAZAR	You chicken-hearted, spineless youth! Do you want the Princess — yes or no? The choice is yours; if not, then go.
ALADDIN	Alright, then. Come on. Open the door — Let's get it over with.
ABANAZAR	You're certain?
ALADDIN	Sure!

(*Underscore. Incantation.*)

ABANAZAR	Omar Khayyam From Nishapur Salaam Salaam Open the Door!

(*Nothing happens.*)

ABANAZAR	Wrong spell — that's plain.
ALADDIN	I think you'd better try again. Surely that's not the only spell you know.
ABANAZAR	Alright, alright, I'll have another go. I'm Abanazar When I knock Abracadabra Open the lock!

(ABANAZAR *knocks three times. Nothing happens.*)

ALADDIN	I reckon I could open it.
ABANAZAR	Oh yes — says who?
ALADDIN	Says me!

(*Rumbling. Then silence.*)

ABANAZAR	That nearly worked, Aladdin. What did you do?
ALADDIN	I just said "says me". (*More rumbling.*) Maybe it's a clue. (*To audience.*) Do you know what the magic words are?

ACT ONE

>(*Probable reply: "Open Sesame". If not,* ALADDIN *can prompt from "says me".*)
>
>Open Sesame! Right. Let's try: "Open Sesame!" After three. One, two, three!

AUDIENCE   "Open Sesame!"

>(*More rumbling. Silence.*)

ALADDIN   Again. One, two, three!

AUDIENCE   "Open Sesame!"

>(*Louder rumbling. Some lightning. Silence.*)

ALADDIN   Nearly. One last time. Really loud. One, two, three!

AUDIENCE   "OPEN SESAME!!"

>(*Louder rumbling. More lightning. Climactic opening.*)

ALADDIN   Wow! Thanks, everyone. Well, here goes!

>(*Exit* ALADDIN *through opening.* ABANAZAR *in spot at side.*)

ABANAZAR   He's in — at last! And when I've got the Lamp
I'll leave him in the Cave, all cold and damp.
Dark and dismal, deep in dirt and slime:
Alone, unheard of till the end of Time!
And you, my friends, who helped me in my plot,
Are part of Aladdin's downfall — like it or not!

>(*Exit* ABANAZAR. *Blackout. Front of cave out.*)

(B) *Inside the cave.*

ALADDIN *appears at the top of the cave. Rough steps down into the cave. As eerie as possible — perhaps flitting shapes, ghosts and ghoulies. Spiders, bats, etc. Craggy. Stalactites dripping with water. As horrible and vile as possible. The lamp must not be visible at this stage.*

ALADDIN *climbs gingerly down the steps.*

ALADDIN   It's not what I expected, Uncle. Uncle — can you hear me?
(*A bat or creepy flies past.*) Ugh! Uncle . . .

ABANAZAR   (*above, at cave entrance*)

	Yes, yes, I'm here. The Lamp: you found it yet?
ALADDIN	Just give me time. It's dark down here. Don't fret. Ugh! It's all slimy and damp. I can't see any jewels or gold. (*Another bat. He may fall the rest of the way down. To audience.*) Is Abanazar playing a trick on me? (*YES!*) Are you sure? (*YES!*) Right —
ABANAZAR	Come on, come on — I haven't got all night.
ALADDIN	I don't trust you, Abanazar. There's no treasure. This is a trap!
ABANAZAR	You'll see it when you've got the Lamp. Simple as that!
ALADDIN	If you're so keen to find this Lamp, come and get it yourself.
ABANAZAR	I can't! The entrance is too small, And I'm too fat and far too tall.
ALADDIN	That's a lie. I'm getting out before it's too late.

(*He starts to scramble up.*)

ABANAZAR	That's what you think, my lad — until you yield And find the Lamp I'll keep this entrance sealed. Three days and nights my prisoner you'll be. Your fate thereafter? Just you wait and see!

(*Manic laughter. Cave entrance shuts just as* ALADDIN *gets there.*)

ALADDIN	No! Don't leave me in this terrible place! Please! (*Pause.*) It's no good, he can't hear me. Maybe if I could find this wretched Lamp I'd know what's so special about it.

(*The lamp glows, behind and above him.*)

Can you see it anywhere?

AUDIENCE	It's behind you!

(*The lamp stops glowing just as* ALADDIN *turns round.*)

ALADDIN	Oh come on, this is no time for jokes.

(*The lamp glows again.*)

AUDIENCE	Behind you!
ALADDIN	Alright. I'll have another look.
	(*The lamp stops glowing.*)
	There's no Lamp!
AUDIENCE	There is!
	(*The lamp glows for the third time.*)
ALADDIN	Where?
AUDIENCE	Behind you!
	(*He looks round and sees it.*)
ALADDIN	You were right! Thanks a lot. I'll see if I can reach it. (*As he climbs or reaches it.*) What a dirty old Lamp!
AUDIENCE	(*probably*) Rub it! Rub the Lamp!
ALADDIN	(*if not*) I think it could do with a good polish. Shall I give it a rub? (*YES!* — ALADDIN *can busk this.*) OK, then — here goes!
	(ALADDIN *rubs the lamp. Flash. The* SLAVE OF THE LAMP *appears.*)
ALADDIN	Crikey! Who are you?
SLAVE	Slave of the Lamp am I. Ready to do or die: Whatever you demand, Your wish is my command!
ALADDIN	Why me?
SLAVE	You're my Master — I obey. Any time, by night or day, Rub the Lamp and I'm your Slave. Tell me what it is you crave.
ALADDIN	I'm famished. What about a take-away?
SLAVE	Yes, Master. (*Calling.*) Chinese take-away for one!

(Enter two children, dressed as waiters, with lavish trolley.)

ALADDIN   I say!

CHILD ONE	One number seven,
CHILD TWO	extra number six,
CHILD ONE	A small eleven,
CHILD TWO	bird's nest soup.
CHILD ONE	Chop sticks?
CHILD ONE	Spring rolls,
CHILD TWO	prawn crackers,
CHILD ONE	lychee,
CHILD TWO	egg fried rice,
CHILD ONE	Pork balls,
CHILD TWO	China tea.
BOTH	Thank you, Sir!

ALADDIN   Very nice!

(Exit Children. ALADDIN *starts tucking in.)*

SLAVE   For what else, Master, do you thirst?

ALADDIN   Hang on, I'm eating. First things first.

SLAVE   My potency is infinite —

ALADDIN   Then take me home.

SLAVE   You mean that's it?

ALADDIN   Yes. Hang on — no! Can you grant me wealth?
I want it for the Princess, not myself.

*(*SLAVE OF THE LAMP *begins to laugh.)*

ALADDIN   Excuse me!

SLAVE   Sorry!

ALADDIN   Come on — what's the joke?

SLAVE   I know that you're a decent sort of bloke
But — well, they all say that. "Give me money,
Not for me, of course." I find that funny.

ALADDIN	For a Slave you've a keen sense of the absurd.
SLAVE	I've seen it all before. But say the word — I'll bring you wealth beyond your wildest dreams. This Cave, O Master, is *not* what it seems!
ALADDIN	Then do it, Slave. That is my demand. Make me rich!
SLAVE	Your wish is my command!

(*Music. During the number, the cave is transformed into a jewelled kingdom. Brilliant and beautiful and stunning! Lights stud the entire cave with gems. In dumbshow, four children enter and present boxes of pearls, gold, gems, silks, etc — all directed by the* SLAVE OF THE LAMP.)

Song: It's A Magical Day (ALADDIN)

ALADDIN
NO ONE EVER BELIEVED IN ME,
NO ONE KNEW WHAT I COULD DO.
NO ONE EVER STOPPED TO SEE
THAT WHAT I WAS SAYING WAS TRUE.

BUT SOMEHOW I OPENED THE DOOR TO THE CAVE,
SOMEHOW I GOT IN.
AND SOMEHOW I FOUND THE WILL TO BE BRAVE,
AND NOW I THINK I'M GOING TO WIN.

IT'S A MAGICAL DAY —
IT'S A NEW BEGINNING.
I'M ON MY WAY —
AT LAST I FEEL I'M WINNING.
I PUT IN MY FINGER AND PULLED OUT A PLUM:
LOOK OUT, WORLD — HERE I COME!

THIS IS MY CHANCE, AND I'M GOING TO TAKE IT.
THIS IS THE DAY — I CAN FEEL IT INSIDE.
NOW AT A GLANCE I CAN SEE HOW TO MAKE IT.
NOW I CAN ASK THE PRINCESS TO BE MY BRIDE.

IT'S A MAGICAL DAY —
A BEAUTIFUL MORNING.
I'M ON MY WAY —
A NEW DAY IS DAWNING.
OUT OF MY WAY, MOVE OVER CHUM:
LOOK OUT, WORLD — HERE I COME!

IT'S A NEW BEGINNING.
I'M ON MY WAY —
AT LAST I FEEL I'M WINNING.
THE DARK CLOUDS HAVE PARTED,
IT'S TIME TO HAVE FUN:
LOOK OUT, WORLD — HERE I COME!
LOOK OUT, WORLD — HERE I COME!

(*A few extra effects may be reserved for the climax to the song — Perhaps the cave entrance opens to a flash.*
ALADDIN *should sing final lines from the entrance, bathed in light from outside. Curtain. Interval.*)

ACT TWO

Scene One

Frontcloth (B): Araby.

Flash. Enter ABANAZAR.

ABANAZAR　　It's me again! Lovely to see you all!
　　　　　　I trust you had a rotten Interval.
　　　　　　I hope your ice creams melt, your toffees stick,
　　　　　　And all that horrid chocolate makes you sick!
　　　　　　Back to the plot: I left Aladdin all alone
　　　　　　Inside the Cave. But when I rolled away the stone
　　　　　　He'd gone. Curses! Perhaps you people know
　　　　　　What's happened to him. Do you? Yes or no?
　　　　　　(*Reaction.*) Useless! Pathetic! So — I'll rub the Ring.
　　　　　　Genie — wake up!

　　　　　　(*Enter* GENIE OF THE RING.)

GENIE　　　　　　　　　　　　Oh! This is sickening!
　　　　　　I'm overworked and underpaid! Okay —
　　　　　　What is it now? I haven't got all day.

ABANAZAR　　Where is Aladdin?

GENIE　　　　　　　　　　Back home. Where d'you think?

ABANAZAR　　What! In Peking?

GENIE　　　　　　　　　　　I thought you'd cause a stink.

ABANAZAR　　Too bad! But tell me — where's the Magic Lamp?

GENIE　　　　Aladdin's got it now, the little scamp!
　　　　　　Such a nice boy. He hasn't lost his head.
　　　　　　Now he'll end up with the Princess instead.

ABANAZAR　　Quiet! Listen to what I have to say.
　　　　　　Fly me to Peking. Now. Without delay.
　　　　　　I'll steal the Magic Lamp. I'll lie. I'll cheat.
　　　　　　And I'll have the Princess. Oh — revenge is sweet!

　　　　　　(*Exit both. Frontcloth out.*)

Scene Two

WIDOW TWANKEY'S *Laundry*.

TWANKEY *is sitting alone, raiding her piggy bank.*

TWANKEY   Hello, dears. I'm down to my last yen and today we're being convicted from the Laundry. I'm so repressed. Aladdin's gone missing, too. I think he must have been abdicated.

(*She starts sobbing, and wipes her nose on the back of her hand, sneeze-style.*)

AUDIENCE   Hanky, Twankey!

TWANKEY   Thank you, dears!

Song: Lament (TWANKEY — *first verse*)

TWANKEY   I'M FEELING BLUE.
WHAT AM I GONNA DO?
THE SKIES ARE GREY,
'COS ALADDIN'S GONE AWAY.

I'M FEELING SAD,
AND AWFUL BAD.
THE CLOUDS ARE BLACK.
WHAT IF ALADDIN DON'T COME BACK?

(*Enter* WISHEE, *with basket. Music continues under following.*)

WISHEE   Watcha Kids!

AUDIENCE   Watcha Wishee!

WISHEE   Watcha Mum!

TWANKEY   I should never have trusted that awful man.

WISHEE   Who, Mum?

TWANKEY   Avabanana.

WISHEE   No thanks — I've just eaten.

TWANKEY   Is that the Palace laundry?

WISHEE   Yes.

TWANKEY   (*sobbing*) The last lot we'll ever do!

Song: Lament (TWANKEY *and* WISHEE — *second verse*)

TWANKEY	I'M FEELING BLUE.
WISHEE	AND I AM TOO!
TWANKEY	WHAT ARE WE GONNA DO?
WISHEE	I HAVEN'T A CLUE!
TWANKEY	THE SKIES ARE GREY.
WISHEE	WHAT A HORRIBLE DAY!
BOTH	'COS ALADDIN'S GONE AWAY.
WISHEE	I'M FEELING SAD.
TWANKEY	I'M FEELING MAD!
WISHEE	AND AWFUL BAD.
TWANKEY	THE WORST DAY I'VE HAD!
WISHEE	THE CLOUDS ARE BLACK.
TWANKEY	WE GOT THE SACK!
BOTH	WHAT IF ALADDIN DON'T COME BACK?

BOTH   OUR LIVES ARE ALL A-CRUMBLING,
                FALLING ROUND OUR EARS.
                OUR HOPES ARE ALL A-TUMBLING,
                DROWNING IN OUR TEARS.

(TWANKEY *continues to sob quietly*.)

WISHEE   The broker's men are coming at three o'clock to take everything away.

TWANKEY   (*sobbing*) I know!

WISHEE   Why are they called broker's men, Mum?

TWANKEY   'Cos they break up your home when you're broke.

(*The clock strikes three*.)

WISHEE   They're late.

(PRINCESS *and* SING SONG, *dressed in boiler suits and caps as broker's men, pop their heads out of the basket*.)

TWANKEY   Yes. Where are they?

AUDIENCE	Behind you! In the basket! (*Etc.*)
TWANKEY	In the basket?
AUDIENCE	Yes!

(PRINCESS *and* SING SONG *duck down as* TWANKEY *and* WISHEE *turn.*)

TWANKEY	Oh no they're not! (*Etc x 3.*) Oh, very well then, I'll have a look. (*She opens the basket.*) Aarrhh! Get out of there, you petty, disreputable, re-possessing pests!

(PRINCESS *and* SING SONG *jump out of the basket and reveal themselves.*)

PRINCESS	Don't worry, Widow Twankey, it's only us!
TWANKEY	(*in awe*) Princess!
WISHEE	(*pleased*) Sing Song!
SING SONG	Watcha Wishee!
TWANKEY	(*bowing and scraping*) Pardon my consumption, your Loyal Highness! I apologise from the heart of my bottom.
PRINCESS	That's alright. We had to disguise ourselves so father wouldn't catch us leaving the Palace.
SING SONG	We've come to cheer you up.
PRINCESS	And to see Aladdin.
TWANKEY	You're very kind, dears. But I'm incontrollable. Aladdin's gone missing.
PRINCESS	Missing!
TWANKEY	He's been kidnapped by Avanothermarsbar. We'll never see him again.

Song: Lament (TWANKEY, WISHEE, PRINCESS *and* SING SONG — *third verse*)

TWANKEY	I'M FEELING BLUE.
SING SONG } WISHEE	AND WE ARE TOO!

ACT TWO

PRINCESS TWANKEY } SING SONG	WHAT CAN WE DO? WE HAVEN'T A CLUE!
WISHEE OTHER THREE SING SONG ALL	THE SKIES ARE GREY. WHAT A HORRIBLE DAY! 'COS ALADDIN'S — GONE AWAY!

(ALADDIN *enters unnoticed. He is dressed like a Prince.*)

ALADDIN   Hi, Ma!

TWANKEY   Hello, Aladdin. (*Then she registers. general jubilation.*) Aladdin! Where did you get those clothes?

ALADDIN   Abanazar's not my uncle, Ma. He left me in the Cave to die, but I found the Magic Lamp and —

TWANKEY   Hang on, hang on — what Magic Lamp?

ALADDIN   I'm telling you, Ma. I'm the richest man in the world.

(*He claps his hands, and two* JEWEL-ATTENDANTS (*as in cave*) *enter, one with the lamp on a cushion, the other with a casket of jewels.*)

I'm going to ask the Emperor for the Princess's hand in marriage.

TWANKEY   Have you been at the cooking sherry again?

ALADDIN   Look — I'll prove it.

(*He rubs the lamp.*)

My Slave appear,
I need you here.
A simple task
Is all I ask.

(*Flash.* SLAVE OF THE LAMP *appears.*)

TWANKEY   Oh, my hat! (*Bowing low.*) Salaam! Salaam! Get down, Wishee!

WISHEE   (*bowing low*) Salaam! Salaam!

ALADDIN   It's alright, Ma. He won't hurt you.

TWANKEY } WISHEE	False alarm! False alarm!
SLAVE	Your Slave am I To do or die. What's your will? You know the drill!
ALADDIN	Grant my mother whatever she desires.
TWANKEY	Well, strike me pink!

(*Pink spot on* TWANKEY.)

Excuse me, dears. I'm having one of me 'ot flushes.

(*Exit* TWANKEY — *quick change.*)

ALADDIN	Slave!
SLAVE	Yes, Master?
ALADDIN	Provide my mother with the richest, finest and most expensive clothes in Peking. And while you're at it, I think she might like you to make her beautiful. Can you do that?
SLAVE	Gorgeous clothes? Okay, that's fine. At facials, though, I draw the line!
ALADDIN	And I want to see the Princess. Please.
SLAVE	Your future bride? Just close your eyes.

(ALADDIN *shuts his eyes and* SLAVE *turns him as* PRINCESS *gets out of her broker's man outfit and stands by him.*)

Now open wide.

WISHEE } SING SONG	Surprise, surprise!
ALADDIN	Thank you, Slave!
SLAVE	I aim to please.

	Such feats as these Are simply done — And rather fun!
ALADDIN	Princess. These jewels are for you.
PRINCESS	Aladdin! They're beautiful!
	(*Re-enter* TWANKEY, *dressed up to the nines. Glam and gaudy.*)
TWANKEY	Hello, dears! Do you like the frock? It's the new racing car look. Hugs tightly round the curves! Now all I need is a man to go with it.
	(*Enter* EMPEROR, *with* PING PONG.)
EMPEROR	Come along, Ping Pong.
TWANKEY	I said a man!
EMPEROR	Where's Widow Twankey? I've come to impound her personals.
TWANKEY	What a gas! He doesn't recognise me!
EMPEROR	All her goods, Ping Pong. Into the skip.
PING PONG	What?
EMPEROR	Skip, Ping Pong. Skip!
PING PONG	Skip. Right.
	(PING PONG *produces rope and starts skipping.*)
PING PONG	Jelly on a plate, Jelly on a plate, Wibble-wobble, wibble-wobble, Jelly on a plate.
EMPEROR	Not skip, you fool — skip! Doh!
SING SONG	(*deep voice*) Don't worry about him, Emperor. We'll take charge.
TWANKEY	(*very deep voice*) Absolutely! (*High voice.*) I mean, absolutely!

EMPEROR	Who are you, Madam?
TWANKEY	I'm Twankey, who do you think?
EMPEROR	And I suppose his name's Aladdin!
TWANKEY	It is, as a matter of fact.
EMPEROR	Do I look like a fool?
PING PONG	Don't answer that, Madam.
EMPEROR	I intend to get to the bottom of this.
TWANKEY	(*goosing him*) So do I!
PRINCESS	It is Aladdin, father.
EMPEROR	Then arrest him, Ping Pong.
PING PONG	Call the police! Call the police!
	(*He hands* EMPEROR *his truncheon.*)
EMPEROR	You are the police, you fool. (*He hits* PING PONG *over the head with truncheon.* PING PONG *falls over.*) Doh!
PRINCESS	Aladdin gave me these jewels, father.
EMPEROR	Jewels?
PRINCESS	He's fabulously rich.
EMPEROR	Fabulously . . . well my boy, you know I always liked you.
TWANKEY	And I'm his richly fabulous mother.
EMPEROR	You shall have my daughter's hand.
ALL	Hurrah!
ALADDIN	I accept, your Highness —
ALL	Hurrah!
ALADDIN	On one condition.

Twankey	Hurrah! — Eh?
Aladdin	That her consent is freely given.
Emperor	So-Shy?
Princess	It is, father.
Aladdin	Slave!
Slave	Yes, Master?
Aladdin	Build for his Highness, Foo Wiff Pong — A brand new Palace second to none. What are you waiting for? Don't be long.
Slave	No sooner said, my Lord, than done!

(*Exit* Slave of the Lamp.)

Emperor	A new Palace — goodie! Ping Pong — put out a Proclamation that the wedding of my daughter Princess So-Shy and Aladdin will take place in three days. That will give me time to find a nice rich widow for myself. (*He gooses* Twankey.)
Twankey	Ooooh! Empy!
Sing Song	Come on, everyone — what are we waiting for? Let's celebrate!

Song: Celebration/Showstopper (*Mainly dance.*)

Full Company (*except* Abanazar *and* Genie)

Sing Song	BRING OUT THE BUNTING! FLY THE FLAGS!
Princess	GET OUT THE CRACKERS!
Sing Song	PUT ON YOUR GLAD RAGS!
Twankey	SHOPPING AND WASHING-UP CAN WAIT.
All	IT'S TIME TO CELEBRATE!
Ping Pong	SOUND THE TRUMPET!
Aladdin	BANG THE DRUM!
Wishee	CRASH THE CYMBALS!
All Three	HERE WE COME!
Emperor	MAKING MUSIC'S APPROPRIATE:
All	IT'S TIME TO CELEBRATE!

Dance: Four main stages.

(1) Led by SING SONG: *Barn Dance.*
(2) TWANKEY: *Can-Can.*
(3) EMPEROR (*with* WISHEE *and* PING PONG): *Sand Dance.*
(4) SLAVE OF THE LAMP: *Spectacular solo spot.*

ALL BRING OUT THE BUNTING!
FLY THE FLAGS!
GET OUT THE CRACKERS!
PUT ON YOUR GLAD RAGS!
SHOPPING AND WASHING-UP CAN WAIT:
IT'S TIME TO CELEBRATE!
LET'S MAKE MERRY — LET'S JUBILATE!
IT'S TIME —
IT'S TIME —
IT'S TIME TO CELEBRATE!

(*They form a Conga to exit, as frontcloth comes in and* ABANAZAR *enters to witness the tail end of the dance.*)

Scene Three

Frontcloth (A): Street in Peking.

Enter ABANAZAR.

ABANAZAR Their celebrations cut me to the quick:
Aladdin and the Princess make me sick.
My cunning stratagem proceeds apace —
This Royal Wedding, friends, will not take place.
Here is my plan: disguised as an old tramp,
Before your very eyes I'll nab the Lamp.
The Princess then will have to marry me.
You don't believe it? Just you wait and see.

(*Exit* ABANAZAR. *Enter* ALADDIN.)

ALADDIN I'm going to marry the Princess. I can't believe my luck. Now I've got to think of an extra-special wedding present for her. I know — I'll ask the Slave of the Lamp.

(*He rubs the lamp.*)

Oh Slave — appear.

ACT TWO

(*Flash. Enter* SLAVE OF THE LAMP.)

SLAVE — Master — I'm here.
Ready still
To do your will.

ALADDIN — What do you give a Princess who's got everything?

SLAVE — Obvious, I should have thought.

ALADDIN — What?

SLAVE — A wedding ring!

ALADDIN — Brilliant! Fetch me a ring rare and beyond price.

SLAVE — This instant, Master. (*Producing it.*) Here!

ALADDIN — Now that's what I call *nice*!

SLAVE — It belonged to a former Master of mine —
Priceless, unique, and of special design.

ALADDIN — It's magic!

SLAVE — You said it! Now, if you'll excuse me —
I haven't quite finished the Palace upholstery.

(*Exit* SLAVE OF THE LAMP.)

ALADDIN — What a fabulous ring!

(*Enter* TWANKEY, *singing*.)

TWANKEY — "I'm getting married in the morning . . ."

ALADDIN — Are you, Ma?

TWANKEY — Well, Empy hasn't actually asked me yet but I think he's going to. I was chatting to my old friend Mother Goose, and she said a very similar thing happened to her here last year. By the way, did you know she's going to be a granny? Jill's expecting goslings — isn't that nice? (*This speech can be adapted to suit the last year's panto — or it can be cut.*)

ALADDIN — Look at this, Ma. It's for So-Shy.

TWANKEY — Oooh — what a lovely ring!

ALADDIN	Will you look after it for me till the wedding?
TWANKEY	It'll be quite safe with me, dear.

(*He gives it to her.*)

ALADDIN	Thanks, Ma. 'Bye everyone!

(*Exit* ALADDIN.)

TWANKEY	This ring could do with a bit of a polish if you ask me.

(*She rubs the ring. Flash. Enter* GENIE OF THE RING.)

TWANKEY	Aarrhh!
GENIE	Look! I'm tired! I'm cross! I'm —
TWANKEY	In a lather!
GENIE	Ooops! Sorry! Thought that you were Abanazar.
TWANKEY	What? Not Abataramasalata?
GENIE	That's him. I'm *not* his greatest fan.
TWANKEY	Me neither. I can't stand the man. I'm Nancy Twankey, by the way — but you can call me Twanks.
GENIE	Genie Ring — just call me Jean.
TWANKEY	Pleased to meet you, Jean my dear. But what exactly are you doing here?
GENIE	Don't you know? You rub the ring: I appear.
TWANKEY	Ooh — it's a Magic Ring!
GENIE	You've got the idea. I tell you it's an awful chore On call all the time.
TWANKEY	Oh, what a bore!
GENIE	And speaking constantly in verse, If anything, is even worse.

TWANKEY Stop speaking in verse then.

GENIE I can't.

TWANKEY Of course you can. Just say something — anything.

GENIE Er . . . Mary had a little lamb —
It's fleece was white as snow,
And everywhere that Mary went —

TWANKEY The lamb went too, but only on Thursdays. See? It's easy. Now I'll start:

Roses are red —
Violets are blue —
Sugar is sweet —

(*Pause.*)

GENIE If you like that sort of thing!

TWANKEY Brilliant! You're cured. And you don't have to stay cooped up in that ring any more, either.

GENIE Who says?

TWANKEY I say. I've got the ring, and . . . (*Singing.*) "I release you, let you go . . ."

GENIE Thank you, dear. You're a treasure.

TWANKEY The pleasure's mine, Jean. But tell me, how did you become a Genie in the first place?

GENIE Well . . .

Song: Now I Am A Genie (GENIE)

GENIE I WAS PUSHING MY TROLLEY ROUND TESCO'S ONE DAY
AND I THOUGHT: WHAT A LIFE, WHAT A DRUDGE, WHAT A BORE.
HOW I WISH I COULD SUDDENLY FLY AWAY
TO A SUN-DRENCHED BEACH ON A FOREIGN SHORE.
AND WHEN I OPENED MY EYES:
IMAGINE — WHAT A SURPRISE!

FOR THERE WAS THE BEACH WITH THE PALM
                              TREES SWAYING,
THE SEA WAS A SPARKLING AZURE BLUE;
AND I THOUGHT: MY GOODNESS — WHAT WAS I
                                  SAYING?
"HOW I WISH I COULD FLY!" — AND MY WISH
                              CAME TRUE!

SO I STAYED FOR AN HOUR, HAD A DIP —
LAZED ON THE BEACH AND WALKED ROUND THE BAY.
THEN I WISHED AGAIN, REVERSED THE TRIP —
AND WAS BACK WITH MY TROLLEY BY THE BAKED
                              BEAN DISPLAY!
AND I THOUGHT: THOUGH IT SEEMS RATHER QUEER —
THAT THIS COULD BE THE START OF A NEW CAREER.

I COULD BE A GENIE —
I COULD MAKE YOU FLY.
I COULD GRANT YOU WISHES —
WELL, AT LEAST I COULD TRY.
I COULD USE MY MAGIC
TO MAKE YOUR DREAMS COME TRUE.
I WOULD HOLD MY HANDS JUST SO,
WAVE THEM TO AND FRO —
THEN BEFORE YOU KNOW, THE SPELL IS SPUN.
OH, BEING A GENIE COULD BE SO MUCH FUN!

TWANKEY	(*spoken*) That's amazing. So what did you do next?
GENIE	AN AD IN THE JOURNAL, I THOUGHT, WAS THE THING: "APPRENTICE MAGICIAN — EXPERIENCE NONE: "SEEKS A POSITION JUST GIVE ME A RING."
TWANKEY	ANY REPLIES, DEAR?
GENIE	ONLY THE ONE. NO PRIZES FOR GUESSING HIS NAME.
TWANKEY	ABANAZAR?
GENIE	THE VERY SAME! ENTRANCED AT FIRST BY THIS HANDSOME STRANGER, TOO LATE! I WAS TRAPPED! I WAS CAST AS HIS SLAVE!
TWANKEY	YOU REFUSED?

GENIE	POINT BLANK, WHEN I SAW THE DANGER. A REFUSAL, MY DEAR, THAT HE NEVER FORGAVE! LOCKED IN THAT RING, YEAR AFTER YEAR, NEVER THOUGHT I'D GET AWAY. TILL YOU CAME ALONG, TWANKS, YOU DEAR — AND RELEASED ME BY MAGIC THIS VERY DAY. AND I THOUGHT, AFTER AGES OF STRIFE, THIS COULD BE A BRAND NEW LEASE OF LIFE! NOW I AM A GENIE, THERE'S NOTHING I CAN'T DO.
TWANKEY	CAN YOU DO MY WASHING?
GENIE	AND THE IRONING TOO! I WILL USE MY MAGIC TO GRANT YOUR EVERY WISH. I WILL HOLD MY HANDS JUST SO, WAVE THEM TO AND FROM — THEN BEFORE YOU KNOW, THE DEED IS DONE.
TWANKEY	OH, BEING A GENIE SOUNDS AMAZING FUN!
GENIE	YES, BEING A GENIE'S REALLY RATHER . . . (*Producing flowers.*) . . . FUN!
TWANKEY	Oooh, Jean — I can see we're going to be great chums. Let's go and have a butchers at the Emperor's new Palace. I need your advice on the fixtures and fittings. That Slave of the Lamp's got dreadful taste.

(*Exit both. Frontcloth out.*)

Scene Four

Palace Gardens.

In the distance, up centre, is the new palace (a cut-out, which will be flown out later). Oriental magnificence. The roof is level in the centre (ready for spire addition — see below).

ALADDIN *with the lamp,* EMPEROR *and* PRINCESS *are on stage.*

ALADDIN	How do you like your new Palace, your Excellency?

EMPEROR	It's magnificent, Aladdin! A palatial prototype of pulchritudinous perfection!
PRINCESS	Father!
TWANKEY	(*off*) Empy!
	(*Enter* TWANKEY *and* GENIE OF THE RING.)
EMPEROR	Such breathtaking beauty!
TWANKEY	(*to* GENIE) I told you he liked me.
EMPEROR	Those classical curves —
TWANKEY	Oh, Empy!
EMPEROR	Those flying buttresses!
TWANKEY	Hang on.
EMPEROR	There you are, Twankey-poo. What about my new Palace, eh?
TWANKEY	It doesn't look finished to me.
EMPEROR	You have my permission, dear heart, to make any improvements you like.
	(*Exit* EMPEROR.)
TWANKEY	Any improvements I like! What a gas! Aladdin — ask that nice young man [in the snakesuit] to come here a moment.
ALADDIN	(*handing her the lamp*) You ask him, Ma. Rub the Lamp.
TWANKEY	Ooooh! May I?
	(*She rubs the lamp.*)
TWANKEY	O Slave! O Slave! Come 'ere, at my behest!
	(*Flash. Enter* SLAVE OF THE LAMP.)
SLAVE	(*fed up*) Okay, okay, I'm here. What's your request?
GENIE	(*to* TWANKEY) Hardly what I call keen!

TWANKEY	(*to* GENIE) My thoughts entirely, Jean.
SLAVE	I may be at your back and call: Don't take me for granted, that's all! (*To* ALADDIN.) Sorry, Master, if I sounded shirty: EastEnders starts at seven-thirty.
ALADDIN	Slave, you're pardoned.
SLAVE	Thank you, Sire. (*To* TWANKEY.) To what, O Lady, do you most aspire?
TWANKEY	Aspire?
SLAVE	A spire, you say? Then "a spire" it shall be. One! (*First stage of spire — as Salisbury Cathedral — appears on Palace.*) Two! (*Second stage of spire — including scaffolding — appears.*) Three! (*Red light on top glows.*) (*This sequence should be adapted to suit a major local landmark.*) (*Exit* SLAVE OF THE LAMP.)
TWANKEY	There must be more to this wishing business than meets the eye. Come on, Jean — we'll leave these two love-birds alone. See you later, dears. If you need us, we'll be in the Palace looking at carpet samples. (TWANKEY, *with lamp, and* GENIE *tiptoe off.*)
PRINCESS	Aladdin — there's something I have to ask you.
ALADDIN	What's that, So-Shy?
PRINCESS	Would you still love me if I wasn't the Princess?
ALADDIN	I've always known there was just one person for me, Princess. Song: *Someone* (PRINCESS *and* ALADDIN)

ALADDIN	SOMEONE TO BE WITH ME,
	SOMEONE TO BE THERE.
	SOMEONE TO BELIEVE IN ME,
	SOMEONE WHO WILL CARE.
	SOMEONE WHO WILL LOVE ME,
	SOMEONE WHO IS TRUE.
	SOMEONE SPECIAL —
	AND THAT SOMEONE IS YOU!
PRINCESS	SOMEONE WHO IS THOUGHTFUL,
	SOMEONE WHO IS JUST.
	SOMEONE WHO IS GENTLE,
	SOMEONE I CAN TRUST.
	SOMEONE WHO IS FEARLESS,
	SOMEONE WHO IS FUN.
	SOMEONE SPECIAL —
	AND I KNOW THAT YOU ARE THE ONE!
ALADDIN ⎱	SOMEONE TO BE WITH ME,
PRINCESS ⎰	SOMEONE TO BE
ALADDIN ⎱	SOMEONE TO BE THERE.
PRINCESS ⎰	WITH ME, SOMEONE TO BE
ALADDIN ⎱	SOMEONE TO BELIEVE IN ME,
PRINCESS ⎰	THERE. SOMEONE TO BE-
ALADDIN ⎱	SOMEONE WHO WILL CARE.
PRINCESS ⎰	LIEVE IN AND CARE.
PRINCESS ⎱	SOMEONE WHO WILL LOVE ME,
ALADDIN ⎰	SOMEONE WHO WILL
PRINCESS ⎱	SOMEONE WHO IS TRUE.
ALADDIN ⎰	LOVE ME. SOMEONE WHO IS
PRINCESS ⎱	SOMEONE SPECIAL.
ALADDIN ⎰	TRUE.
ALADDIN	SOMEONE SPECIAL.
BOTH	SOMEONE TO LOVE ME,
	AND THAT SOMEONE IS YOU.
	THAT SOMEONE IS YOU!
ABANAZAR	(*off*) Spare some change.

PRINCESS   Till tomorrow, Aladdin.

ABANAZAR   (*off*) Spare some change.

                  (*She blows him a kiss and exits.*)

ALADDIN   Till tomorrow, Princess.

                  (*Enter* ABANAZAR.)

ABANAZAR   Spare some change — a few yen if you can;
                  Spare some change, mister, for a poor old man.

ALADDIN   Here's gold.

ABANAZAR   I thank you! Blessings on your head!

ALADDIN   God be with you!

                  (*Exit* ALADDIN.)

ABANAZAR   Would that he were dead!
                  Now watch my subtle plot unfold:
                  Bargain sale! New lamps for old!
                  Swop them for the latest range —
                  New lamps for old — a fair exchange!

                  (*Enter two children with old lamps, perhaps a small broken anglepoise and a hurricane lamp. Out of a large satchel* ABANAZAR *takes new lamps — small but gaudy replicas of the Magic Lamp. He gives them to the children in exchange for theirs.*)

                  It's working! See how gullible they are!
                  A few loss leaders!

CHILD ONE   Thank you!

CHILD TWO   You're a star!

                  (*Exit children.*)

ABANAZAR   Ugh! Kids! How loathsome! (*Calls.*) Bring your lamps to me!
                  Trade in your old ones — get a new one free!

                  (*Enter* PING PONG *with an old Dixon of Dock Green-type blue lamp.*)

PING PONG   Give me something for this one, mate.
Bit more modern, and up-to-date.

(ABANAZAR *produces new police lamp with flashing unit.*)

ABANAZAR   One I made earlier.

PING PONG   Wow! Thanks a lot!

(PING PONG *runs off, making siren noises.*)

Da da da da da da da —

ABANAZAR   What a clot!
New lamps for old!

(*Enter* EMPEROR *with Magic Lamp.*)

EMPEROR   My friend —

ABANAZAR   (*aside*) He's got it!
Gently, Abanazar bit by bit . . .

EMPEROR   This belongs to my future son-in-law.
Can't afford a wedding present. Therefore —
Since he's been very generous to me
I thought a brand new lamp —

ABANAZAR   Now let me see.
Rather inferior, but never mind —
I suppose it will do.

(*They exchange lamps. The* EMPEROR *might get* PING PONG'S *old one back.*)

EMPEROR   You're very kind.

(*Exit* EMPEROR.)

ABANAZAR   Mine at last! Aladdin's curst!
Powers of darkness — do your worst!
Universal potency I crave.

(*He rubs lamp.*)

Come forth thou foul, malingering Slave!

(*Flash. Enter* SLAVE OF THE LAMP.)

SLAVE	What's your will?
ABANAZAR	Shut up, and listen to me. Uproot that Palace there immediately And fly it straight away to Araby.
SLAVE	Anyone in it, Master?
ABANAZAR	Yes — the Princess. I want to cause her maximum distress. I'll have her for my slave, and then my wife. Should she refuse — she'll answer with her life.
SLAVE	Could I avoid this charge, I'd find a way. But you're my Master, and I must obey.

(*Thunder, changed lighting, etc. Palace ascends, trailing roots and foundations.* ABANAZAR *and* SLAVE OF THE LAMP *exit. Re-enter* EMPEROR.)

EMPEROR   What's going on? What's going on? Help! Ping Pong! Help!

(PING PONG *rushes on with his new siren lamp flashing on his head.*)

PING PONG   Clear the streets! Don't panic! Women and Emperors last!

EMPEROR   Look! My lovely new Palace!

PING PONG   Where's it gone, your Thin Airship?

EMPEROR   Search me.

PING PONG   Search you? OK!

(*He quickly frisks* EMPEROR, *who is very ticklish.*)

EMPEROR   Doh!

(ALADDIN *and* WISHEE WASHEE *run on.*)

ALADDIN   What's happened, your Highness?

WISHEE   What's happening? What's happening?

EMPEROR	My new Palace has disappeared, that's what. If this is your idea of a joke, Aladdin, I am not amused. I knew I should never have trusted you. Ping Pong — put on the handcuffs.
PING PONG	Put on the handcuffs. Right.

(PING PONG *puts handcuffs on the* EMPEROR.)

EMPEROR	Not on me, you fool! Doh!
ALADDIN	Wait — please. Tell me what happened — *exactly*.
EMPEROR	Well, I'd just given your old Lamp to this tramp —
ALADDIN	Abanazar! There's no time to lose! Where's the Princess?
WISHEE	And Sing Song?
EMPEROR	And Twankey-poo?
PING PONG	And Jean?

(*Enter* GENIE OF THE RING, *with carpet.*)

GENIE	Here I am, dear. I was just looking at carpet samples. But I'm afraid the other three were in the Palace. Abanazar's whisked them away to his dreadful Den in Arabia.
ALADDIN	We must all go and rescue them.
EMPEROR	But it's miles to Arabia! Miles!
GENIE	I used to be quite hot on travel. You could say it's my forte.
PING PONG	You're what?
GENIE	Forte.
PING PONG	Amazing — you don't look a day over thirty.
GENIE	I'll fly you to Arabia.
WISHEE	Fly?
GENIE	There's room for one on this Carpet, for a start. (*She lays down on the carpet.*) On you get, your Highness. Age before beauty!

EMPEROR	Doh!
GENIE	Hurry up —
EMPEROR	I think Aladdin should travel on the carpet: not that I'm afraid or anything, but —
WISHEE	I agree. Aladdin should go first. He's by far the bravest.
ALADDIN	What about the rest of you?
GENIE	Don't worry. I'll think of something. Come on, there's no time to lose! (ALADDIN *gets on.*) Now for the magic words, if I can remember them . . .

Magic Carpet
Through the sky,
Something something —
Carpet: fly!

(*Nothing happens.*)

There's a magic word missing in the middle.

WISHEE	My mates here might be able to help.
GENIE	Good idea, Wishee. Can anyone think of a good magic word?

(*Audience may suggest Abracadabra. If not, use what they do suggest.*)

Abracadabra! I think that's it. Let's try.

(*During the following verse the lights dim and blacks come in behind. Lighting appropriate to the Magic Carpet established.*)

Magic carpet
Through the sky,
Abracadabra —
Carpet: fly!

(*Slight movement.*)

WISHEE	I saw it move that time. Maybe if we all joined in, that might make the spell work. All together —

(WISHEE *and the others lead the audience: the verse is repeated. More movement.*)

Nearly! Third time lucky. Really loud this time!

(*The verse is repeated. The carpet takes off. Overlapping lines as follows and/or ad-libs as desired.*)

ALADDIN	I'm flying, Wishee! See you in Arabia!
GENIE	We won't be far behind!
PING PONG	Careful when you meet Abanazar!
WISHEE	Give my love to Sing Song if you see her first!
EMPEROR	Lots of love to Twankey-Poo!
ALL	'Bye, Aladdin! 'Bye!

(*Frontcloth in.*)

Scene Five

Frontcloth (B): Araby.

Enter ABANAZAR, *with* PRINCESS *as prisoner.*

ABANAZAR Back in Araby — the Lamp is mine!
Universal power — how divine!
Riding high — my strength is absolute.
My prize, the Princess! Ain't she cute!

PRINCESS Never, Abanazar, will I yield.

ABANAZAR Sorry, darling heart, your fate is sealed!
My prisoner for ever you will be:
My slave, my lovely little chickadee.

PRINCESS No slave of yours, you brute! I'd rather die.

ABANAZAR (*to audience*) She doesn't like me much — I wonder why!
You like me, don't you?

AUDIENCE No!

ABANAZAR	Oh yes you do!
AUDIENCE	Oh no we don't!
ABANAZAR	Oh yes you do!
AUDIENCE	Oh no we don't!
ABANAZAR	Oh yes you do!
AUDIENCE	Oh no we don't!
ABANAZAR	Oh.. . . very well then! I hate you too!
PRINCESS	Aladdin will rescue us. Have no fear.
ABANAZAR	Don't kid yourself: he'll never find you here. Besides, my dear, he wouldn't last long.
PRINCESS	Aladdin's all-powerful —
ABANAZAR	That's where you're wrong: He had the power for a day or two: Now he's lost the Lamp, it's just me and you!
PRINCESS	You don't frighten me: you think you're so tough. You're just a lightweight, a coward —
ABANAZAR	Enough! Any more cheek — I'll take you down the Nile And feed you to my favourite crocodile! Evil is my aim — all goodness I'll destroy; And any brat who misbehaves, girl or boy, Will be force-fed rat stew in frog-spawn sauce, With grilled cat, on a bed of mice, for second course! Delicious . . . Silence! Though you hiss and boo, You can't hate me as much as I hate you. So, my friends, welcome to my little Den — One opens it to the public now and then. (*Frontcloth out: action into Scene Six is continuous.*) And meet my two new slaves, who should be working. Come on, you idle layabouts — no shirking!

Scene Six

ABANAZAR's *den in Araby.*

Egyptian feel. Walls covered in red, orange, brown, gold (etc) hieroglyphics. Figures of ancient Egyptians. Tomb chamber: there are five full-sized, upright mummies. Four are simply movable cut-outs (though they should look as much like the fifth as possible) which can be moved (eg, wheeled) easily forward, concealing the person behind. The fifth, and middle, mummy contains the SLAVE OF THE LAMP, *though this should come as a surprise. He must be able to walk and raise his arms, etc (and get hold of a cup), and he has to 'escape' from the costume in a flash. (This can be cheated: on his final appearance he can have a false front which can be discarded easily). The five mummies are spaced evenly round the den. Either side of the central mummy are two panels: secret swing doors. In front of this mummy is a bench, which should overbalance one end when nobody is sitting on the other. The Magic Lamp is locked in a safe (big padlock), prominent and visible — the lamp can be seen behind bars (but on no account should it look easily accessible).*

TWANKEY *and* SING SONG *are mopping the floor —* ABANAZAR's *slaves.*

Four children as slave-attendants fanning with palms.

SING SONG	We'll escape, you coward, just you wait.
TWANKEY	How about a tea-break sometime mate?
ABANAZAR	When *I* say, skivvy — not before. Want to live? Then mop that floor! Total power — nothing do I lack.
TWANKEY	Only a brain!
ABANAZAR	Shut up, you —
TWANKEY	Oh, me back!
ABANAZAR	At my mercy — what a treat. In my power — oh, revenge is sweet!

Song: Double-Dealing Rotter (ABANAZAR, *with* TWANKEY, SING SONG *and* PRINCESS *as backing vocals)*

ABANAZAR	I'M A DOUBLE-DEALING ROTTER, WITH ICE FOR A HEART — UH, HUH, HUH!
CHORUS	OOO WAH! OOO WAH!

ABANAZAR AND I'M AN EVIL-MINDED PLOTTER AND I'M
          READY TO START —
          UH, HUH, HUH!

CHORUS   OOO WAH! OOO WAH!

ABANAZAR TO CONQUER THE UNIVERSE IS MY PLAN —
          UH, HUH, HUH!

CHORUS   OOO WAH! OOO WAH!

ABANAZAR AND I'M GONNA MAKE IT HAPPEN JUST AS SOON
          AS I CAN —
          UH, HUH, HUH!

CHORUS   OOO WAH! OOO WAH!

ABANAZAR WELL I DON'T CARE IF YOU SCREAM AND CURSE,
          'COS I'M THE WICKEDEST MAN IN THE UNIVERSE —
          UH, HUH, HUH!

CHORUS   OOO WAH! OOO WAH!
          OOO WAH! OOO WAH!

ABANAZAR WELL SOME FOLKS THINK I'M REALLY BAD —
          UH, HUH, HUH!

CHORUS   HE'S BAD, REAL BAD!

ABANAZAR AND SOME WOULD EVEN SAY I'M MAD —
          UH, HUH, HUH!

CHORUS   HE'S MAD, RAVING MAD!

ABANAZAR BUT I DON'T REGRET A THING I'VE DONE —
          UH, HUH, HUH!

CHORUS   WHAT A ROTTER, OOH WHAT A ROTTER!

ABANAZAR IT'S BEEN THE MOST DELIGHTFUL FUN —
          UH, HUH, HUH!

CHORUS   WHAT A NUTTER, AN UTTER NUTTER!

ABANAZAR YOU CAN SCREAM AND SHOUT UNTIL YOU DROP,
          BUT NOTHING'S GONNA MAKE ME STOP —
          UH, HUH, HUH!

Chorus	HE'S BAD — OOH, WHAT A ROTTER! HE'S MAD — AN UTTER NUTTER!
Abanazar	(*to* Princess) YOU'RE SWEET, BUT I'M SWEETER! (*to* Sing song) YOU'RE NEAT, BUT I'M NEATER! (*to* Twankey) YOU CAN'T COMPETE WITH ME FOR CHARM AND PERSONALITY!

(*Dance break.*)

Abanazar	YOU WANNA BE IN MY GANG, MY GANG, MY GANG? YOU WANNA BE IN MY GANG?
Chorus	NO WAY!
Abanazar	I DON'T CARE IF YOU SCREAM AND CURSE, I'M THE WICKEDEST MAN IN THE UNIVERSE! YOU CAN SCREAM AND SHOUT UNTIL YOU DROP BUT NOTHING'S GONNA MAKE ME STOP. MY PLANS TO RULE THE WORLD HAVE JUST BEGUN — AND NOTHING, NOTHING, NOTHING'S GONNA STOP ME HAVING FUN!
Abanazar	I feel like a snooze. Princess, come with me. I only trust you under lock and key, If this floor hasn't got a perfect sheen When I come back — I'll make you lick it clean!

(*Exit* Abanazar, *dragging* Princess. *Children also exit.*)

Twankey	What a nasty man. I hope he gets ants in his pants!
Sing Song	And smellies in his wellies!
Twankey	And piranhas in his pyjamas! Come and sit down dear, and take the feet off your legs.

(*They sit simultaneously at opposite ends of the bench. The* Mummy *is close behind them, visible to the audience in the space between them.*)

Sing Song	We need to think.
Twankey	A drink? Good idea.

(*She gets out a flask with mug top, pours a measure, and passes it along.*)

There you go.

(*The* MUMMY *intercepts it, drinks it all, and passes the cup along to* SING SONG.)

SING SONG   Thank you. Er . . . (*She passes it back.*) Widow Twankey . . .

TWANKEY   My, you are thirsty. (*Pouring another.*) Have another.

(*Same business.*)

SING SONG   Thank you. Er . . . (*Passing it back again.*) Widow Twankey . . .

TWANKEY   I think you've had enough, dear.

SING SONG   But . . .

TWANKEY   Oh, alright. But that's your lot. (*She pours another.*)

(*The* MUMMY *drinks for a third time. This time, as he passes the cup on to* SING SONG, *she sees him and runs off through the false door with a scream. The* MUMMY *follows her off. As* SING SONG *gets up,* TWANKEY *falls off the bench.*)

TWANKEY   Well, really! (*She notices that* SING SONG *has gone.*) She's gone and left me all alone! (*To audience.*) Did you see anything? (*A Mummy.*) My Mummy? Don't be silly. . . (*No, etc.*) Your Mummy? (*No, etc.*) Where is it now then, this Mummy? (*The* MUMMY *has returned . . . Behind you! etc.*) Alright, I'll have a look.

(*Two false circles. Finally she sees it. The* MUMMY *chases her off through one of the false doors. Then out from the other one and off again. Then, third time,* TWANKEY *is chasing the* MUMMY *around and off. Enter* EMPEROR, *disguised as a nineteenth century British explorer, followed by* ALADDIN *and* GENIE OF THE RING *dressed as Egyptian assistants.* (*False beards, fezzes, etc.*) *Much tiptoe, bumping into each other, "shhh!" acting.*)

EMPEROR   Aladdin?

ALADDIN   (*pulling down his false beard*) Yes!

EMPEROR   Jean?

GENIE	(*pulling down her false beard*) Yes!
ALADDIN	There's the Lamp!
GENIE	Under lock and key.
EMPEROR	Don't worry. I've thought of a plan.
ALADDIN GENIE }	You have?!
ABANAZAR	(*off*) Who's there?
ALADDIN EMPEROR GENIE }	Shhh!!

(*Enter* ABANAZAR.)

ABANAZAR	Who are you? How dare you enter my Den Without permission? And who are these men?
EMPEROR	My assistants. I'm Major Forster-Stand — Famous explorer. Let me shake your hand.
ABANAZAR	What do you want?
EMPEROR	To entertain you, Sire.
ABANAZAR	What do you mean?
EMPEROR	I'll set your heart on fire! One thing I learnt in the Bengal Lancers: Never travel without a couple of dancers!

(*He claps his hands.*)

Fatima!

(*Enter* WISHEE.)

Very Fatima!

(*Enter* PING PONG. *Both are dressed as dancing girls in the full "turkish delight" garb. Outrageous exotic eastern dancing.*)

ABANAZAR	(*at end of dance*) These maidens don't half appeal to me! I'll have them as wives Numbers Two and Three!
	(*Appalled reactions from* WISHEE *and* PING PONG.)
ABANAZAR	As for you and your miserable sidekicks, you will die — *Unless* you can help me with a problem. Will you?
EMPEROR	I can try.
ABANAZAR	You're an explorer?
EMPEROR	Forster-Stand — that's me!
ABANAZAR	I have a little local difficulty. This Den is haunted by the Mummy's curse. It's always scared me — now it's getting worse. Whoever meets this Mummy face to face Will disappear, they say, without a trace — Into thin air! Destroy it for me — fast, Unless you want this day to be your last!
	(*Exit* ABANAZAR.)
EMPEROR	Ping Pong!
PING PONG	Yes, Major?
EMPEROR	You'll have to do it!
PING PONG	What's that, Major?
EMPEROR	Bump off this crumbling Mummy, you bumbling dummy!
PING PONG	With respect, your Majority — I am engaged to be married to Abergavenny. I have to save meself!
EMPEROR	Doh!
ALADDIN	Never mind the Mummy — where's the Princess?
WISHEE	And Sing Song?
ALADDIN	And talking of Mummies —
ALADDIN WISHEE	Where's ours?

(*Enter* TWANKEY.)

TWANKEY	Here I am, dears. (*She kisses them. To* EMPEROR.) Who are you?
EMPEROR	I'm Forster-Stand.
TWANKEY	I am sorry! Some kind of accident?
EMPEROR	Doh!
TWANKEY	I'd know that 'Doh!' anywhere! Empy!
EMPEROR	Twanks!

(*Enter* SING SONG.)

SING SONG	Wishee!
WISHEE	Sing Song!
ALADDIN	Where's the Princess, Ma?
TWANKEY	She's been taken prisoner by the awful Avadramarama. He's going to force her into macrame against her will.
EMPEROR	We'll die if we don't find this Mummy.
ALADDIN	We must get the Lamp. Where does he keep the key?
TWANKEY	Round his neck . . . hang on: what Mummy?
ALADDIN	There's a curse. If you meet the Mummy, you disappear.
TWANKEY	Don't be ridiculous. I've met him. He's ever so nice. I'll seduce you to him. (*She calls.*) Mummy! I think he's a bit shy. (*To audience.*) Will you help us, dears? (*Yes.*) After three — One, Two, Three.
ALL	Mummy!
ALADDIN	A bit louder. One, Two, Three . . .
ALL	Mummy!
TWANKEY	Third time lucky. One, Two, Three . . .
ALL	Mummy!!

(*Enter* MUMMY, *very shy.*)

ALL — Ahhh!

TWANKEY — Hello, dear. We're in a spot of bother — will you help us?

(*The* MUMMY *nods.*)

Empy — tell us what to do.

EMPEROR — Right. This is what we'll do. (*He whispers to* WISHEE *and* SING SONG.)

WISHEE — You don't say! (*He whispers to* PING PONG.)

PING PONG — You don't say! (*He whispers to* GENIE.)

GENIE — You don't say!

TWANKEY — (*to* GENIE) What do we have to do, Jean dear?

GENIE — I don't know — he didn't say!

ALADDIN — It's obvious. Abanazar's terrified of the Mummy, right? (ALL: *Mmmm.*) So when he comes back, the Mummy can creep up on him — very slowly. (ALL: *Mmmm.*) He'll be petrified — frozen with fear. Then we can get the key, take the Lamp, and rescue the Princess. (ALL: *Yes!*)

WISHEE — We could all hide behind the other Mummies and join in.

SING SONG — Brilliant, Wishee!

GENIE — That'll make it even more scary.

TWANKEY — Still not scary enough. We need some sound effects. I know! (*To audience.*) Would you make scary noises at the same time? (*YES!*) When I give the signal — like this. (*Scary signal.*)

(*Scary noises from audience.*)

WISHEE — Well — that was quite good but you can be much more creepy than that —

TWANKEY — And grisly —

EMPEROR	And ghastly —
GENIE	And gruesome —
PING PONG	And eerie —
SING SONG	And weird —
ALADDIN	All right, all right I think they've got the point!
TWANKEY	Let's have another go. Remember — only when I give the signal. (*Signal: response.*)
ALADDIN	Fantastic! You scared *me* that time.
ABANAZAR	(*off*) What's going on?
ALADDIN	Quickly! To your posts!
	(ALADDIN, GENIE, PING PONG *and* WISHEE *go behind the four mummies. The* EMPEROR *stays out.* TWANKEY *and* SING SONG *start dusting mummies. Enter* ABANAZAR, *with* PRINCESS.)
ABANAZAR	What's going on? What's all this dreadful noise? I hope it's not you horrid girls and boys. (*To* EMPEROR.) You still here? I told you: find that Mummy.
EMPEROR	I've a funny feeling in my tummy: Don't look round — the cursed Mummy's *here*!
ABANAZAR	Oh no! Not here! I'm paralysed with fear. I'll lose my magic powers — it can't be true —
EMPEROR	Say your prayers! He's coming to get you!
	(TWANKEY *gives signal to audience. Scary sounds. If audience begins earlier, don't discourage them. No matter if lines are lost — plough on!*)
ABANAZAR	There's more than one of them. I can see five!
EMPEROR	They're surrounding you!
ABANAZAR	Aarrhh! And they're alive!
EMPEROR	Sorry, mate — it's not your lucky day.
ABANAZAR	(*collapsing*) Stop! I surrender! Please please go away!

ALADDIN	He's going!
ALL	Going! Gone! Hurray!
TWANKEY	Aladdin — get the key from round his neck.

(ALADDIN *goes for the key, and then unlocks the lamp safe.*)

Empy — you were wonderful!

EMPEROR	Thankey, Twankey!
PRINCESS	I hope he hasn't died of fright.
PING PONG	No — he's still breathing. He's alright.
ALADDIN	I've got it, Ma!

(ALADDIN *rubs the lamp.*)

ALADDIN Slave appear
Wherever you are.
I need you here —

(*Flash.* SLAVE OF THE LAMP *appears from the mummy.*)

SLAVE	Tarantara!!
TWANKEY	Him all the time in alabaster!
SLAVE	What's your will, O mighty Master?
ALADDIN	I want to thank you, Slave, for all you've done. I grant you here, in front of everyone, Any one wish you want — I proclaim it.
SLAVE	Anything, O Master?
ALADDIN	Yes — you name it.
SLAVE	My freedom, Master.
ALADDIN	What?
SLAVE	My freedom.

PRINCESS	Aladdin — you promised.

(*Pause.*)

ALADDIN	Slave go free. Take your lamp. Go your way.
SLAVE	For the last time, Master — I obey.

(SLAVE OF THE LAMP *takes lamp and goes.*)

TWANKEY	You must be mad, Aladdin. You've given away your power.
ALADDIN	We're still rich, Ma. I've got the Princess —
EMPEROR	And I've got you, Twankey-poo!
TWANKEY	You have?
EMPEROR	Oh marry me, marry me you adorably delicious little damson!
TWANKEY	You don't mean it?
EMPEROR	I do. Call me a fool, but I'm mad about you.
TWANKEY	You're a fool — but I'm mad about you too! Alright, I'll marry you, but on one condition.
EMPEROR	What's that?
TWANKEY	We can have rabbit beer at the reception.
EMPEROR	What's rabbit beer?
TWANKEY	The same as ordinary beer. Only it's got more hops in it.
ALL	Doh!
WISHEE	All this talk of weddings is really boring. I want to go home.

(ABANAZAR *begins to come to, groaning.*)

EMPEROR	What about old Abracadabra here?

TWANKEY	I'll need a servant when I'm the Empress! Come on Jean — do your travel bit . . .
GENIE	Nowadays my powers are slight — I hope I get the magic right.

(*She takes centre stage as lights start to fade and the others fall back.*)

Spirits, guide us through the night,
Faster than the speed of light.

(*Frontcloth slowly in.*)

Close your eyes and keep them tight
Settle down — enjoy your flight.

(*Blackout by now. Spot on* GENIE. *Frontcloth in.*)

Bing-bong!

Thank you for flying "Genie of the Ring."
Shortly we'll be landing in Peking.
Refreshments were provided by Widow Twankey, but nevertheless we hope you enjoyed your flight.

Thank you!

(*Spot out. Exit* GENIE.)

Scene Seven

Songsheet — Frontcloth (A)

NB: *This scene is scripted to give a suggested structure but it can be changed as desired.*

Enter SING SONG.

SING SONG	I'm really fed up! Now the Princess is getting married to Aladdin, and the Emperor's getting married to Widow Twankey, I'll be left all alone. I'm so sad.
AUDIENCE	(*fed by band if necessary*) Aaah!
SING SONG	I'm much sadder than that.

AUDIENCE	Aaaaahhh!
SING SONG	And who'll be landed with the extra housework? Yours truly! It'll be:

(*Spoken in steady rhythm.*)

Change your socks
And clean the bath —
Tidy your room
And weed the path. (*Band starts to punctuate.*)
Feed the cat and *dust* the chande*l*iers.
And don't forget to wash behind your ears!

Hey — that would make rather a good song.

(*She sings it again, with full band support.*)

That's really cheered me up! Tell you what — will you sing it with me? (*Yes.*) Will you? (*YES!*) Thanks.

(*She begins. They don't know it.*)

AUDIENCE	(*perhaps*) We don't know the words!
SING SONG	You don't know the words, do you! Well, it just so happens . . . (*The words descend.*) Right — all together!

(*She sings it with the audience.*)

Well, that was quite good, but I reckon there were some grown-ups not singing. Look — if there's a grown-up sitting next to you not singing or doing the actions, give them a poke in the ribs. One more time, with the actions this time!

(*They sing it again. Enter* WISHEE.)

WISHEE	(*gloomy*) Watcha Kids!
AUDIENCE	Watcha Wishee!
WISHEE	(*even gloomier*) Watcha Sing Song.
SING SONG	What's the matter, Wishee?

WISHEE	I'm really fed up. Now Aladdin's getting married to the Princess, and Mum's getting married to Foo Wiff Pong, I'll be left all alone. I'm so sad!
AUDIENCE	(*fed by* SING SONG) Aaah!
WISHEE	I'm much sadder than that.
AUDIENCE	Aaaahhh!
WISHEE	And who'll be landed with the extra housework? Yours truly! It'll be:
	(*He starts to speak the verse in rhythm*: SING SONG *and audience join to make it the song.*)
WISHEE	Hey! How did you know that?
SING SONG	Well, I was feeling a bit miserable too, Wishee, and all my friends here have been cheering me up.
WISHEE	I want to sing it with you. (*Close to her.*) I do love a good Sing Song.
SING SONG	(*pleased and embarrassed*) Oh, Wishee!
WISHEE	(*not understanding*) What?
SING SONG	Forget it! Come on then, let's sing it again. All together!
	(ALL *sing again.*)
WISHEE	That was brilliant. But do you know, Sing Song — I couldn't hear a single grown-up. My mates were much louder, weren't we, kids?
AUDIENCE	YES!
WISHEE	And we'll prove it. We'll try something never before tried in the history of British panto. We'll have a competition. Shall we do that, kids?
AUDIENCE	YES!
SING SONG	Alright Wishee, but I think the grown-ups should go first.
WISHEE	Fine, fine. Age before beauty.

Sing Song	Cheeky thing. Right grown-ups. Here we go:

(*Grown-ups sing with* Sing Song. Wishee *scornful.*)

Wishee	Have you started? (*Etc.*) We can do better than that, can't we kids?
Audience	YES!
Wishee	Right — here goes!

(Wishee *sings with the kids.*)

Wishee	We won! We won! We won!
Sing Song	We need a judge. (*To pit.*) Maestro: may we have marks out of ten, please. First, for the grown-ups.

(M D *shows a card with 6, then reverses it to 9.*)

Wishee	And for the kids.

(M D *shows 1, then adds 0 to make it into 10.*)

Sing Song	Alright — just to show there are no hard feelings, let's all sing it together. Extra loud, one last time!

(*All sing again. Words fly out during verse.*)

Both	'Bye! 'Bye!

(*Exit* Wishee *and* Sing Song. *Frontcloth slowly out.*)

Scene Eight

Palace Gardens. (Walkdown.)

Added reds, golds and silvers, certainly in costumes. Chinese lanterns. Wedding celebration. Enter the six children: brief formal dance. Bow.

Enter Genie of the Ring.

Genie	It's time to part — our panto's done. It's years since I've had so much fun. Aladdin and So-Shy — married today. Pity their Palace had to fly away!

(*Enter* SLAVE OF THE LAMP.)

SLAVE For an ending, that's not very pleasant.
Palace: re-appear!

(*The finished palace flies in at the back. Extra central pagoda completes it: no spire now.*)

      A wedding present!
I'm free. I have to fly.
I take my bow —

GENIE   And so do I!

(*They bow together and break to sides. Walkdown in the following order.*)

EMPEROR *and* PING PONG

ABANAZAR

WISHEE *and* SING SONG

TWANKEY

ALADDIN *and* PRINCESS

ALADDIN (*to audience*) Welcome, friends — our wedding guests!

ABANAZAR Them? The loathsome little pests!

TWANKEY Now, now Abby: remember what you said.
You promised to be nice.

ABANAZAR   I wish I were dead!

SLAVE That could be arranged —

TWANKEY   Decease! Both of you!
No squabbling. Now then, Empy-poo —
My tummy's wobbling! Today's a *double* wedding day!

(*She kisses him.*)

WISHEE A treble! Sing Song —

(*He kisses her.*)

GENIE	Quadruple! Ping Pong!

(She kisses him. Increasing company reaction to the three kisses.)

Song: Finale. Celebration (reprise) ALL

ALL
BRING OUT THE BUNTING!
FLY THE FLAGS!
GET OUT THE CRACKERS!
PUT ON YOUR GLAD RAGS!
SHOPPING AND WASHING UP CAN WAIT.
LET'S CELEBRATE!

SOUND THE TRUMPET!
BANG THE DRUM!
CRASH THE CYMBALS!
HERE WE COME!
LET'S MAKE MERRY, AND STAY UP LATE!
LET'S CELEBRATE!

SING SONG Our panto's over for another year.

ABANAZAR I love you all!

TWANKEY Don't overdo it dear!

WISHEE See you soon —

ALADDIN It's time to go.

ALL Happy Christmas (New Year)! Cheerio!

(Frontcloth in. Playout.)

Scene Four (A)

U V Sequence (Blackcloth)

Note: *This is an entirely optional sequence, to go between the magic carpet take off and the Araby frontcloth before the den. It was not included in the first production.*

Cut-out locations:

(1)   Great Wall of China

(2)   Taj Mahal

(3)   Mt Everest

(4)   Araby (Pyramids)

These can be interspersed with clouds, signposts, comic birds, directions to Gooseland, etc, etc.

The travellers:

(A)   The Palace. Uprooted. Perhaps Flag with "HELP!!"

(B)   ABANAZAR and SLAVE OF THE LAMP on giant lamp — like jet plane (Magic Lamp Airlines.)

(C)   ALADDIN on Magic Carpet.

(D)   EMPEROR, GENIE OF THE RING, WISHEE and PING PONG: "Flying Squad". Some kind of comical police-plane.

Notes:

The direction of the travellers should be the opposite from the direction we have seen the 'real' carpet travelling.

Main principle: the locations move faster than the travellers, to give the impression of the travellers moving. Therefore the locations can be relatively far apart and interspersed with signposts, palm trees, parrots, camels, etc, etc. Obviously, the travellers move in the opposite direction from the locations.

In the same direction as the travellers (either at the same speed or overtaking or being overtaken) can be clouds, birds, Priscilla the goose, etc, etc.

The sequence:

(A)   Great Wall (breaking above principle, and going quite steadily).

(B)   Palace flies over.

(C)   ABANAZAR and SLAVE OF THE LAMP in hot pursuit.

(D)   Palace off.

(E)   ABANAZAR and SLAVE OF THE LAMP off.

(F)   Carpet over wall.

(G)   Flying squad, following, over wall.

(H)   Wall off, as:

(I)   Carpet and flying squad (LC and RC) 'stop' and the following locations cross more rapidly than wall did:

(J)   Taj Mahal.

(K)   Mt Everest.

(L)   Araby/pyramids.

(M)   Carpet and flying squad off.